The
SELF-LOVE
SUPERPOWER

About the Author

Tess Whitehurst teaches magical and intuitive arts in live workshops and via her online community and learning hub, the Good Vibe Tribe Online School of Magical Arts. An award-winning author, she's written ten books, which have been translated into more than eighteen languages. She has appeared on the Bravo TV show *Flipping Out* as well as morning shows on both Fox and NBC, and her writing has been featured in *Writer's Digest*, *Spirit and Destiny* (in the UK), and online at elephantjournal.com.

TESS WHITEHURST

The SELF-LOVE SUPERPOWER

THE MAGICAL ART OF APPROVING *of* YOURSELF (*NO MATTER WHAT*)

Llewellyn Publications
Woodbury, Minnesota

FIRST EDITION
First Printing, 2021

Book design by Samantha Peterson
Cover design by Shira Atakpu
Editing by Marjorie Otto

Llewellyn Publications is a registered trademark of Llewellyn Worldwide Ltd.

Library of Congress Cataloging-in-Publication Data (Pending)
ISBN: 978-0-7387-6752-9

Llewellyn Worldwide Ltd. does not participate in, endorse, or have any authority or responsibility concerning private business transactions between our authors and the public.

All mail addressed to the author is forwarded but the publisher cannot, unless specifically instructed by the author, give out an address or phone number.

Any internet references contained in this work are current at publication time, but the publisher cannot guarantee that a specific location will continue to be maintained. Please refer to the publisher's website for links to authors' websites and other sources.

Llewellyn Publications
A Division of Llewellyn Worldwide Ltd.
2143 Wooddale Drive
Woodbury, MN 55125-2989
www.llewellyn.com

Printed in the United States of America

Other Books by Tess Whitehurst

Unicorn Magic (2019)
You Are Magical (2018)
The Magic of Trees (2017)
Holistic Energy Magic (2015)
Magical Fashionista (2013)
The Magic of Flowers (2013)
The Art of Bliss (2012)
The Good Energy Book (2012)
Magical Housekeeping (2010)

CONTENTS

ACTION STEPS (EXERCISES)

Disclaimer

The material in this book is not intended as a substitute for trained psychological advice. Readers are advised to consult their personal healthcare professionals regarding any counseling needs. The publisher and author assume no liability for any actions that may occur from the reader's use of the content contained herein.

Acknowledgments

Gratitude to Ted Bruner, Molly Kate Seifert, Linda Konner, and Jonathan Kirsch. Gratitude also to Natasha Levinger, Melissa Tipton, and Tanya Carroll Richardson. In this solitary business, it's good to have coworkers. And, of course, many thanks to everyone at Llewellyn for your help with this book and for your long-suffering support of my career. Finally, the biggest of all thank yous to Patrick: this one's for you.

INTRODUCTION

This book was inspired by a really bad birthday.

Last year, the week after my birthday rolled around, I shared on my podcast that I was so depressed on my birthday that I refused to go anywhere and, in fact, stayed in bed all day reading and crying. It wasn't until the next day, when my partner pretty much dragged me out of bed and into the car for a day trip, that I began to cheer up and get my energy back.

The following week, a podcast listener emailed to express her surprise that someone like me—i.e., someone who is always writing books and blog posts about positivity and manifesting the life of your dreams—would still experience such a thing.

After I read the email, it hit me that I've left something out of my books up to this point—something important. I've neglected to sufficiently illustrate the "imperfect" nature of my personal path. And in the process, I've neglected to sufficiently illustrate the "imperfect" nature of the spiritual path in general, which is synonymous with the path of self-compassion, self-approval, and self-love.

The truth is that none of us have this positivity thing mastered. All of us wake up depressed some days. Show me someone who isn't susceptible to a miserable mood, and I'll show you an action figure, or a cartoon character, or a mannequin. I don't care if you're Eckhart Tolle, Oprah, or the Dalai Lama—if you're a living person on Earth, you'll have moments when you feel vulnerable, self-critical, angry, mopey, irritated, and afraid. You'll go to a party and you'll feel like the odd person out. You'll go over and over something you said and worry that it sounded stupid, or whiney, or self-absorbed. You'll have moments when you're certain that no one likes you and you suspect everyone's been whispering mean things about you behind your back.

That's called being human.

Of course, being human can also involve feeling so much love or perceiving so much beauty you feel like your heart might burst. And the human experience can also include less extreme (but still completely wonderful) positive experiences, like feeling serene, centered, generous, hopeful, masterful, and calm.

And in my experience, there's one thing that can help us navigate the challenging aspects of this life and cultivate the pleasant and transcendent ones more than any other single thing. That's self-love. When you learn to have compassion for yourself throughout it all and to forgive yourself for your imperfections and mistakes—and even to have patience with yourself when you *don't* have compassion for yourself or forgive yourself—everything in your life will benefit. And I mean *everything.*

As you'll hear me say again and again throughout this book, learning to love yourself is a process. It's a journey, not a destination. It's a spiral, not a line. By the end of this book, you won't necessarily be a pro at self-love (because who is?), but you *will* be a pro at experiencing the *journey* of self-love. You'll be a pro at leaning into challenges and breathing through pain. You'll be a pro at having patience with your learning process and responding to problems and mistakes with self-care instead of self-loathing or self-criticism. And you'll discover that this makes all the difference in the world.

Each chapter contains practical action steps. I highly recommend that you take them. It might be tempting to skip over some of them and just read the book straight through, marathon-style. But if you do that, you'll be missing out. You'll be dipping your toe in the water but never diving in. I've designed the exercises and rituals to help you integrate the information in an experiential way. So there will be moments as you're reading this book that you'll want to put the book down for a bit so you can complete the action steps. Have fun with the exercises and approach them with a spirit of experimentation. And if an assignment seems extra tempting to skip for one reason or another, that' a good indication that it will be especially empowering for y' to perform. So get curious about the mysterious blessings h ing behind the reluctance or boredom or fear (or whatever i' and let that curiosity be an incentive to be proactive and p through. You'll be glad you did.

Thank you for taking this journey of self-love with me. I am honored to be your (imperfect) guide.

Love always,
Tess

P.S. I completed this book right before COVID. I'm just letting you know for context, and so it doesn't seem curious that I make no references to the world-altering events of 2020 or 2021.

One
SELF-LOVE: WHAT IS IT?

Every day, we get so many messages. And that's a massive understatement.

Online and in every other form of media, we receive message after message: not just about how we should feel about ourselves, but also about how we should file our nails, pluck our eyebrows, select produce, do a HIIT workout, find a yoga instructor, maintain a marriage, grow an indoor herb garden, ask for a raise, set a table, eat vegan, eat paleo, eat keto, grow our social media following, and the list goes on.

When the message is not explicit, it is often implicit: commercials imply that we should look a certain way or live up to a certain ideal. Articles imply that one way of living or thinking or eating is normal and correct while all alternate ones are fatally flawed. Instagram influencers imply that our house (or pores, or linen shirts, or abdominal muscles, or fruit salad) should look as effortlessly perfect as theirs. And even when we *know* all of these implications are born of illusion, or spin, or propaganda, we can still end up feeling hopelessly inferior.

All of this is simply a monetized, digitized version of what we humans have naturally done to each other for millennia. We are a hierarchical species that sets up and seeks to adhere to power structures and cliques to feel safe, to feel like we are part of a powerful group, and to feel like we belong.

It's often said that such human behavior begins and becomes the most quintessential and obvious when we are in middle school or junior high. I don't know about you, but I remember it starting for me as early as preschool. I have a clear memory of being on the playground and looking at three girls who were probably four to my three, because in my memory they towered above me. The ringleader was wearing a cute outfit and gleaming with charisma and confidence, and said, "Hey, Tess, let's play a game. *We'll* be all the winners and *you'll* be all the losers." Then (at least according to this memory) the girls on either side of her looked down at me and laughed, and I felt ashamed. I didn't know what I could change about myself in order to fit in, but if I had known, I would have changed it.

But even when no one is purposely trying to feel superior or trying to make us feel inferior, we can actually do a pretty good job of tearing ourselves down—with no help from anyone else. For example, have you ever gone to a party where you knew very few people? You probably got the strong feeling that everyone else knew each other, that they were laughing at inside jokes you didn't know, and that they were all somehow more comfortable in their skin than you could ever be. When in fact, all along, everyone else was likely thinking the same exact thing: that *they* were the odd man out and that *you* were one of the comfortable ones, and probably a beloved member of a posh inner circle they didn't know about. This is a natural tendency of humans: by default, we often assume *we* are the weird one, the unloved or unlovable one, the one whom no one really likes.

Of course, narcissism is also a thing. So is self-absorption. There are certainly people with an unwarranted degree of self-confidence and people who filter everything through their belief that they are at the center of the Universe: that everything revolves around them. But this isn't self-love.

Self-love doesn't mean thinking you're the best thing that ever happened to fashion, or art, or the music business, or your favorite dating app. Self-love doesn't mean knowing you have a smoking hot body, or you've got relationships all figured out, or people should want to shower you with gifts, or the world owes you special favors simply for being your fabulous self.

Self-love means believing you have a right to be here, that you have a right to take up space here on Earth: right now, exactly as you are. Self-love means valuing your own happiness over what the world tells you about who you should be or how your life should look. Self-love means listening to your needs and taking care of yourself with love. It's speaking kindly to yourself. It's creating a home that helps you feel comfortable, powerful, and nourished. It's getting into habits that help you feel good about yourself: not so you'll look or be something different than who you are now, but so you'll be proud to be who you are, and celebrate yourself, without apology or embarrassment (although you *are* human, so sometimes you'll still feel embarrassment).

One of my favorite authors, the late Louise Hay, wrote, "We are all here to transcend our early limitations, whatever they were. We're here to recognize our own magnificence and divinity no matter what *they* told us." She also wrote, "Love is the miracle cure. Loving ourselves works miracles in our lives."[1]

The thing about love is that it is infinite. You can never top out when it comes to love. No matter how much you already love yourself, you can always love yourself even more. And the more you love yourself, the happier you will be and the more powerful you will feel.

If you've been berating yourself and being harsh with yourself for a long time, you might worry that being kind and loving to yourself will let you off the hook. You may believe you'll never improve without constant criticism. Actually, the opposite is true.

Have you ever taught very young children? I have. For years, I taught gymnastics and dance to children between the ages of three and nine. I quickly learned that the best way to encourage children to learn was to encourage them—period. Not, "Point those ugly toes," but, "Great work, Victoria! Now let me see you point your toes. Oh, so pretty!" We are the same. Forget the criticism of others for a second: when we live in fear of our *own* criticism, it paralyzes us. We get stuck in patterns we don't enjoy and find it more difficult to improve in areas we care about. But when we encourage ourselves with love and don't demand immediate perfection, we improve much more swiftly and with much more ease. But even more importantly: life feels better! *Much* better. And isn't that sort of why we wanted to "improve" in the first place—to feel better? So why not start there?

Consider the lyrics to the song "Row, Row, Row Your Boat." We've all heard it a million times, but maybe it caught on because its wisdom is so profound.

---

1. Louise Hay, *You Can Heal Your Life* (Carlsbad, CA: Hay House, 1999), 48, 32.

Perhaps no metaphor is as accurate a description of life as *a dream*. Your actual experience of life has no substance: it's a perception in your mind. (Think about it: can you actually prove that it's anywhere other than that? Nope. You can't.) And when you die, your life as you know it, along with all your thoughts and memories as you know them, will disappear and evaporate into thin air—very much like what happens to a dream at the moment you wake up. So, honestly, what is the point of being harsh with yourself? While you're here in this dreamlike existence, why should you row through your life with anything other than gentle merriness, enjoying the scenery, the fresh scent of the wildflowers, the mellifluous sound of the clear mountain stream? And when less pleasant conditions seem to arise in the dream you call your life, why not approach them with compassion and patience? Why not learn to be your own friend and support system? Why not love yourself as best you can, at every bend in the stream, at every step along the way?

While you are likely sold—at least intellectually—on the idea that we are not here to impress other people or to feel superior to them, you may still believe that the planet needs saving: that we need to be harsh with ourselves so we can finally save the environment, end racism, rescue animals from factory farms, and so on. But the truth is, you can do the most good for the planet and your fellow earthlings when you start by loving and treasuring yourself. You can still do the work you feel called to do, but when you do it from a place of universal forgiveness for yourself, you will naturally treat others with similar kindness, and you will be so much more effective in creating positive change.

Here are some of the reasons self-love increases your potential to bring healing and harmony into the world:

- Self-love helps you hear your intuition more clearly, which will alert you to the most powerful way to bring about positive change in any situation.

- Self-love means respecting and believing in yourself. This naturally makes you appear more credible in the eyes of others.

- Self-love carries over into the way you view and interact with others, so it helps you express your opinions without getting into the defensive, us-against-them mentality, which so often erodes effectiveness in conversations, negotiations, and relationships.

- Self-love naturally fills you with genuine excitement and enthusiasm for the things you care about. (What's even better than coffee for boosting morale? Self-love ... *and* coffee. I mean there's no reason you can't have both.)

When you consider all these benefits, you can see that nothing makes more sense than learning to love yourself as you are. Once you get the hang of it, everything else gets *way* easier.

Even though most of us have picked up the habit of harsh self-criticism and likely even self-loathing, we can make a spiritual practice out of learning to love ourselves. We can open up to our own divine nature, forgive ourselves for our mistakes and perceived shortcomings, and become gentler and gentler and merrier and merrier as we row gently down the miraculous stream that is this dream of life.

When you step onto the path of self-love, you will begin to establish a beautiful momentum. You will still have fluctuations in your mood and perspective, and challenges will still arise, but in general, your life will flow better while constantly becoming more and more fun. You'll awaken to your natural ability to create positive change according to your intentions. Doors of opportunity will open more and more frequently. You'll notice beauty everywhere, and you'll focus on it, and what you focus on will expand.

Like so many of us, I have criticized myself quite a lot in my life. At times, I've even loathed and detested and punished and *hated* myself. These feelings may still come up for me on occasion, which is why I've made a lifelong project out of shifting into self-love again and again and again. I'm sorry to break it to you, but learning to love yourself isn't like learning to ride a bike. It's like learning something that you just keep learning and learning unendingly, like coding, or child-rearing, or quantum physics.

But the endless nature of learning to love yourself is not actually a bad thing. It just means that as long as you're alive, you'll be presented with opportunities to learn to love yourself even more. So by definition, it's not about perfection. It's just about showing up and doing your best.

And that's what you're already doing, right now, by reading this book. So take a moment now to appreciate yourself for starting this journey with the following action step. (Please don't skip it! Actually, as I mentioned in the introduction, please don't skip any of the action steps in this book! Each one will create a positive shift and help you internalize the wisdom in a deeper way.)

Action Step
• INVOKE AND INTEND •

Place one hand on your heart and one hand on your belly. Take full breaths, as deeply and as slowly as you comfortably can. Then, just begin to notice your breath. Notice as you breathe in.

Notice as you breathe out. Notice how, when you simply place your awareness on your breath, your breathing naturally begins to deepen, and your body naturally begins to relax. Now say to yourself, "Thank you. I appreciate you for starting this journey. I love you." And if it doesn't feel authentic yet to say, "I love you," say instead, "I am willing to love you. I know in my heart of hearts that you are lovable, and I am willing to open up to seeing you with eyes of love."

Now, call on the Divine in a way that feels powerful for you. Perhaps you feel comfortable with the calling It God, Goddess, Infinite Intelligence, or the Universe. If you're an atheist, you can imagine the Divine as the unified field: the choreography of oneness that weaves it all together into one mesmerizing cosmic dance. No matter what you like to call the Divine, remember that you are one with It. Just as a single wave is part of the ocean or a single spark is part of a fire, you are one with All That Is. Theoretical physicists talk about the Universe as a holograph. Something that makes a holograph a holograph is the fact that every individual piece of it contains the entirety, sort of like the way a single strand of your DNA contains the coding for the entirety of you. So you, by virtue of being in the Universe, actually *contain* the Universe within your every atom and every cell. You don't have to understand this idea logically (I certainly don't), but take a moment to let it percolate. Breathe it in. Marinate in the poetry of it. Let it permeate your consciousness by osmosis.

Once you call on the Divine, ask for help with loving yourself. From your heart, say something simple such as, "It's my intention to love myself, and I'm not really sure how to do that, but I know that You can help, and I know that I am part of You, and that I contain You within my every cell. Please guide me through this process. Please show me signs and messages and help me to be open to them. Please support me in opening up my awareness to my own beauty, and power, and perfection. Thank you."

Action Step
• MAKE A SELF-LOVE ALTAR •

I recommend that you set up a simple altar to serve as a visual affirmation as you move through the chapters and exercises in this book. This can be placed on any flat surface that feels right to you: a small table, a shelf, or even a corner of a countertop. Follow your intuition and creative impulses about what to place on your self-love altar, but as a general guideline, select one item that will represent your relationship with the Infinite, such as a statue of a goddess or god you connect with, or something more secular such as a crystal, a plant, or a framed postcard depicting the stars. That one item is the only necessary prerequisite for any altar, but if you'd like to add additional items, choose things that symbolize self-love for you, such as a heart-shaped crystal, a fresh pink rose in a small vase, words or phrases that inspire you, or a picture of you being hugged by a loved one when you were a child. Keep in mind that an altar possesses an alive, creative energy, so tend to it regularly by dusting it, removing wilted flowers, and lovingly rearranging it from day to day as you feel guided to keep it harmoniously attuned to your intention to love yourself.

Quick note: I am assuming that much of your self-love journey and work will take place in your home, and for that reason, having a designated and symbolic place to do your self-love work (i.e., your altar) can be helpful and fun. But you certainly don't need an altar in order to perform the exercises. If you would like to do some of the action steps while you're on vacation or on a break at work (for example), you could choose a crystal or another small item that feels powerful for you that you can fit in a pocket or purse. That way, you can keep this small anchor item on your altar when you're home and pull it out when you're on the road, as needed, in lieu of your altar.

Be patient with yourself as you move through this journey. You're creating a new habit, establishing a new groove, and over-writing a lifetime of contradictory conditioning. But also keep in mind that learning to love yourself is something you can abso-lutely do, especially when you connect with the powerful force that underlies and defines all things, which is also known as Infinite Love, and which is Who You Really Are. Even if tapping into this love seems out of reach at this moment, rest assured: it isn't. In fact, it's your true identity, which you ultimately couldn't escape even if you tried.

Action Step
• INTENTION TUNE-IN •

Before we move on to the next chapter, find yourself a beautiful journal, or just a fresh notebook you're excited to write in. In it, answer the following questions. Freewrite your answers; don't be precious about it. Don't try to be clever or eloquent. Just let your pen move and your thoughts, feelings, and ideas flow out. Keep writing without stopping until you've filled at least half a page answering each of the three questions:

1. Why did you pick up this book? What brought you here? Describe the moment or realization or tipping point when you decided you wanted to love yourself more. (It's okay if you just saw the book and it called to you. Write about the

moment of attraction. Did the cover catch your eye? Or maybe the title? Why? What was the feeling, exactly?)

2. What would it feel like if you loved yourself unconditionally? How would it feel if you didn't have to be perfect? How would it feel not to live in fear of your own criticism of yourself? Let go of the need to answer this "correctly," and just allow yourself to freely imagine and guess.

3. Who is one person or animal companion you completely adore? What do you love about this person or animal? Is it how good-looking and amazing they are? Or is it something else that transcends their degree of perfection or fabulousness in the eyes of the world?

Two
NOW IS THE ONLY TIME

We all have an ego. A useful way to define the ego *is the illusion that you are separate.* Even though you are one with every other human, and one with the planet, and one with the very power that brought the entire Universe into being, your ego tells you, "No, you are a singular being that is totally separate from everyone and everything."

The ego tells you lots of other things that aren't true. Basically, any time you hear a message in your mind that contributes to your sense of separation, that is your ego talking. *A Course in Miracles* says the ego's basic doctrine is, "Seek but do not find."[2] So you can also think of the ego as that voice in your mind that is

---

2. Helen Schucman, *A Course In Miracles* (New York: The Foundation for Inner Peace, 1976), Lesson 71.

always looking for things that are "wrong," or "unfair," or "holding you back." The ego likes to tell you that if only things were different than they are—if only *you* were different than you are—everything would be great. Of course, by definition, the ego will never be satisfied. There will never be a moment when it will say, once and for all, "You've made it. You're golden. And now everything is going to be great forever."

Your ego will continue to chime in throughout your lifetime, but you might say that the spiritual path is the process of learning, more and more, how to disbelieve the things the ego tells you, and to prefer the truth: that you are one with All That Is, that you can trust the way your life is unfolding, and that you already have everything you need.

Here are just a few of the many, *many* lies the ego likes to tell you:

- You are better than everyone here.
- You are worse than everyone here.
- You should be ashamed of yourself.
- You should feel special.
- You should have come much farther by now in your career.
- Everyone is jealous of how far you have come in your career.
- No one will respect you because your skin looks so bad today.
- Everyone will admire you because your skin looks so radiant today.
- You've already got everything figured out.

- You have a lot of work to do if you're ever going to love yourself and find inner peace, and it's going to take a long, long time.

As I said, these are lies. Not a single one of these things is actually true, or empowering, or helpful in any way. They are all just stories that have no actual bearing on reality. But for now, let's take a look at the final bullet point. Let's consider the tale our egos like to spin about how we have *so much* inner work to do, and how it's going to take *forever*, and how it's going to be *hard*.

When you consider that the ego's objective is to perpetuate itself by keeping you feeling separate, and lacking, and bolstering this sense of separation and lack in any way it can, you can see how clever this story really is. If self-love is feeling naturally worthy, and present, and connected to All That Is, it's in the ego's interest to keep you believing that self-love is only a vague possibility: if it exists at all, it exists far in the future, and requires a great deal of *work*, even though it's unclear exactly what that work might entail.

The truth (though the ego will always vehemently deny it) is this: there is only one moment. And that moment is now.

In this moment, right now, as you read these words, you *can* love yourself. In fact, now is the *only* time you can open up to the part of you that is infinite, eternal, and truly powerful: the part of you that is one with All That Is. You have that power—not tomorrow, not next week, and not at New Year's on the stroke of midnight. You have that power *now*.

The ego is forever soliloquizing—contradicting you, contradicting itself. It never stops. It is saying, "Yeah, but …" and "Yeah right—" and "You're better than that," and "You're not quite there yet," and "You should be ashamed." The trick is not to engage with the ego. Don't identify with it: it isn't you. Don't try to reason with it: it can't be convinced. And don't try to shut it up: it will get even louder. Instead, let it blab away, but realize it isn't you. And then realize that it doesn't have to be the dictator of your inner world. Demote it. Stage a coup. Get it out of the driver's seat. Kick it off the throne.

When I was about twenty years old, a girlfriend and I attended a Rainbow Gathering (an immense, sprawling, pop-up sort of homegrown hippie festival) in the White Mountains of Arizona. Before we drove back to the Grand Canyon, where we were working at the time, we took LSD. While my friend quietly drove her little car along the sparsely populated, two-lane highway, I gazed toward the sunset and darkening sky from the passenger seat while my ego voice proceeded to get so loud, I actually feared I was going crazy. "You don't even know what you're doing with your life! You're bussing tables at a National Park and living in a dorm room. You have no car. You have no prospects. You have no plan. Your family doesn't understand the choices you're making, and neither do you. Face it: you *could* be something special, and you *should* be! But in reality, you're a nobody from nowhere. You're not that pretty, you're not that interesting, and you have practically no money to your name. So what are you going to do about it? Figure something out. *Now*."

Believe it or not, this actually wasn't the drugs talking. This was what my ego was *always* telling me: same old inner monologue, cranked up to eleven. At this volume, it was all but unbearable, and I began panicking when I couldn't figure out how to shut it up. I tried arguing, I tried contradicting, I tried shushing, I tried appeasing, and the resulting escalation of mind volume only made me want to scream and cover my ears.

Just when I thought my sanity was going to fall off the ledge and plunge to a spectacular death, a miracle happened. Something I now know as my Higher Self, or the part of me that is one with All That Is, reached down into my vicious mental conflict and pulled me right up out of it. The ego kept right on berating me, but suddenly I could clearly see that I didn't have to get caught up in it anymore. It was like I was helicoptered out of the eye of the hurricane that was raging within my skull. From this safe place, I could look down at all the horrible things the ego was saying, and smile. The ego hurricane went right on raging, but what it was saying didn't really matter anymore. Actually (I realized), it had never mattered in the first place.

In that moment, even though I wouldn't have articulated it this way, I knew I wasn't my ego. My ego wasn't me. The voice in my head was just noise.

As we continued rolling along the highway under the late summer sunset's radiant oranges and purples, my ego's volume increased again, and I got caught up again. But this time, when I began to panic, I smiled as I remembered I could simply lift my consciousness up and out of the fray.

This happened again … and again … and *again*. Every time, the voice began to feel unbearable, and then, remembering, I smiled. And each time I became less and less ensnared in the ego's bullying voice and more and more identified with the vast, open emptiness that both contains and animates all things.

You definitely don't have to do a hallucinogen to disengage from your ego. It is absolutely, 100 percent, not necessary to take any kind of drug in order to step up and out of your mind's endless diatribe. (And in fact I wouldn't recommend it.) My experience on that Arizona highway was simply an amplified, condensed version of what you can do right now. You can begin the minute you notice you're identifying with or giving any sort of credibility to your ego.

At that moment, simply recognize the monologue in your head for what it is: a disembodied voice that says crazy things, and that seems to have endless criticisms and opinions that have no bearing on anything real, or useful, or empowering. Understand: you are not that voice. You usually don't even like that voice, so there's no reason to either identify with it or respect it. But you don't have to hate it, either. You can simply realize that it isn't personal; it's just noise.

Next, remind yourself that your *actual* consciousness is the same consciousness that is All Consciousness. It is quiet, still, wise, and open. It doesn't berate you and it doesn't tell you how special you are. It simply allows all things to arise and disappear within its quiet openness. That is who you really are. That aspect of you—the true aspect—has never been born and it can never die. It is infinite, eternal, and awake.

You are the sky, not the pollution, or the airplanes, or even the clouds. *You are the sky.*

Another way to identify with this true part of yourself is to ask: who is noticing this voice? Who is the one observing it?

Once this inner shift in perspective occurs, will your ego shut up, finally, and give you some peace? Will it stop berating you, or telling you you're special, or listing all the things it thinks are wrong, or trying to make you feel separate in any way it possibly can? No. Your ego will keep doing all those things. But you will see it for what it is and stop feeding it your life force by believing it is you. When you remove your life force from the ego, and stop identifying with it, it weakens. Over time, its power over you will fade and it will become easier and easier to see it for the pathetic imposter it actually is.

Eventually, you will have hours, days, or even weeks when the voice takes such a back seat, you barely notice it at all, and you are free to concentrate on living your life as it is, without giving as much as the time of day to the relentless narration and irrational spin.

What's more, when you repeatedly remind yourself to step out of the ego and into the present moment, you will begin to see this appearance of form that we call "you" with eyes of love. Here is this human who was born here on Earth—this adorable little being with your name and your face and your story—who is doing the best she can. Who is opening his heart to feeling love: for himself, other people, and this mysterious life experience. Who is already lovable, who is already joyful, and who is already free.

Before you move on to the next chapter in this book, make sure you take the time for the following exercise.

Action Step
• TAKE A WALK •

For this exercise, you're simply going to take a solitary walk during daylight hours, on a pleasant city or small-town street or a rustic natural trail. Spend some quality time and notice what you see and experience: the flora, the fauna, the buildings, and all the scents, sights, and sounds. Notice the feeling of your feet on the earth and the feeling of your breath moving in and out of your body. Every time you notice your inner monologue beginning to distract you in any way from your present moment experience and immediate surroundings, simply smile to yourself. Remove your attention from the ego voice and return it to the earth beneath you, the sky above you, and the sensory beauty that surrounds you.

Remember this: every time you notice your inner monologue taking over, it's a success! It's never a failure. Every single time you shift your focus to the present moment, the ego will weaken, and your connection with your Higher Self will become stronger. *Every time.* So the more the better!

Of course, in everyday life, we will have times when listening to our inner monologue makes sense: for example when we are balancing our finances, discussing a novel with a friend, deciding the next step to take in our career, or planning an event. But when we learn that we are not our inner monologue, even these things become easier because we have created the space for Divine Consciousness (which is who we really are, and which can see the big picture) to flow in and cocreate with our linear, logical mind. At this point, our thinking mind acts like a useful app rather than destructive malware.

Ultimately, when we put the mind in its place, we see that that's all it is: an app. It helps you navigate the day-to-day events and responsibilities of this life. But it isn't who you are. You are Infinite Consciousness in temporary human form. You are a channel of the pure love of creation. You are the Universe, playing within the illusion of form. You are Infinity, dancing to the music of time, celebrating Itself.

After you've taken your walk outside—either immediately after or in the next day or two—try the next action step.

Action Step
• TAP INTO GUIDANCE •

Sit comfortably near your self-love altar with your notebook and a pen. Light a candle or otherwise create a meditative mood, and make sure you won't be disturbed for twenty to sixty minutes. Take some deep breaths, center your mind, and settle in.

When you feel calm and clear, at the top of a page, write, "What new habits or healthy behaviors will benefit me at this time?" Take some conscious breaths and see if you can notice your ego chiming in. You will know it's your ego voice because it will be either critical or self-aggrandizing. For example, if it's critical, it may say things like, "You should stop being so lazy," or if it's self-aggrandizing it may say things like, "You should show the world how great you really are." Don't fight this inner monologue. Just notice it.

Next, imagine you are leaving the ego voice where it is and actually lifting your consciousness up and out of it into a spot a foot or two above your head. From here, ask yourself again, "What new habits or healthy behaviors will benefit me at this time?" Tune into the energy of love. See yourself as a precious human and know you are always doing the very best you can at every moment. Feel forgiveness for your perceived faults and compassion for all your past challenges. From this place of unconditional self-approval, listen deeply for the answer to your question, and write down any clear guidance you receive.

You may receive guidance as words or sentences that arise in your mind, pictures or inner visions, an emotion, or a clear and inexplicable sense of just knowing. However your guidance arrives, trust it and transcribe it into language as best as you can. If you find it difficult to tap into this guidance, or to trust what you are receiving, you can ask yourself, "What if I *could* tap into this guidance? What would it say?" Often, taking a hypothetical approach clears the pressure so you are free to experiment and to believe that what you are receiving is real.

Be aware that when you tune into this channel of wisdom, which is your true identity as the Infinite Intelligence of the Universe, the guidance you receive may not always seem linear or related precisely to your question. Or it may! Just don't place any expectations about content of the guidance.

What you *can* expect, however, is that the guidance you receive will be completely loving, compassionate, and supportive. It may ask you to change your habits, but it will never do so in a critical or judgmental way. It will also be characterized by humility. In other words, it will not compare you to others by emphasizing your inferiority or your superiority. This is because to Universal Wisdom, hierarchy isn't real and is therefore a complete nonissue. From the perspective of Universal Wisdom, every human soul is learning at their own pace, in perfect timing. And everyone is equally wonderful and equally deserving of love.

Once you transcribe the answers you receive for the first question, feel free to repeat the process with other questions. For example, you might ask any of these questions or similar ones:

- How can I begin to love myself?
- How can I love myself even more than I do now?
- How can I forgive myself for _____?
- How can I begin to love and approve of my body (or appearance)?
- How can I let go of anxiety or worry?
- How can I let go of negative self-talk?

- What guidance will help me believe in myself and my value?
- What guidance will most help me accept and approve of myself as I am?

When you feel a sense of completion, review your questions along with the answers that came through, and consider ways to integrate the wisdom you've received. You may want to write a list to remind yourself of the important points, and place it on your self-love altar, refrigerator, near your mirror, or somewhere else that feels right.

You can come back to this exercise whenever you want to lift yourself out of the ego monologue and into the clear stream of wisdom that is always available to you from your True Self, who is one and the same as the Divine Presence, or Infinite Intelligence, or whatever you want to call it.

Three
HOW TO BE KIND TO YOURSELF

By nature, humans are kind. We love giving. We love helping. We love being of service. Just think of the last time you did a favor for someone, whether it was a friend, a family member, or a total stranger. I'm willing to bet it put a spring in your step for the rest of the day.

Sure, the news likes to report sensationalist stories about violence and general unrest. But the reason those stories are so sensational is because they are the exception to human nature rather than the rule. And if you were able to look behind the shocking headline and into the inner workings of the situation being reported, you'd likely see that it was born out of pain. That the primary player in the drama (even if it is a world leader who is perpetuating a violent conflict) was someone who, at some point in their life, was in desperate need of kindness that they didn't receive.

The kindness that you naturally love bestowing on others likely doesn't seem as natural when it comes to yourself. But it can become that way! Being kind to yourself is simply a habit, like any other. And it's absolutely one you can adopt.

In her excellent book *Self-Compassion: The Proven Power of Being Kind to Yourself*, researcher Dr. Kristin Neff illustrates that being kind to ourselves has proven healing benefits on our bodies and minds. She shares this mindful affirmation we can stop and say to ourselves whenever we experience suffering of any kind:

> This is a moment of suffering.
> Suffering is a part of life.
> May I be kind to myself in this moment.
> May I give myself the compassion I need.[3]

The best way to understand this affirmation's effectiveness is to try it right now.

Action Step
• CULTIVATE SELF-COMPASSION •

Place a hand on your heart and the other hand on your belly. Take some deep breaths and then allow your breath to be natural as you place your awareness on the inhale and the exhale. If your

---

3. Dr. Kritin Neff, *Self-Compassion: The Proven Power of Being Kind to Yourself* (New York: HarperCollins, 2015), 119.

breath wants to be shallow, let it be shallow. If it wants to deepen, let it deepen. Whatever you notice about your breath, just allow it to be. Send presence and support through your hands and into your body. Now, bring to mind some area of suffering in your life. It can be little (like a mosquito bite), moderate (like embarrassment over something you said yesterday), or big (like a breakup or the loss of a loved one). Whatever comes to mind first is probably best. Feel the suffering fully. Let it in.

Inwardly, or aloud, say, "This is a moment of suffering."

Notice how simply acknowledging suffering is a relief in itself. You aren't ignoring it or distracting yourself from it or trying to push on in spite of it. You're letting it be what it is: suffering.

Say, "Suffering is a part of life."

I think this one is my favorite. It reminds me that no one—*no one*—gets through life without bug bites, or embarrassment, or grief. Not a single supermodel, prime minister, brain surgeon, or best-selling author in the history of the world has ever escaped (or *will* ever escape) pain, discomfort, irritation, fear, shame, anxiety, and heartbreak.

Say, "May I be kind to myself in this moment."

Now that you've acknowledged the suffering and acknowledged it's part and parcel of being a human on Earth, gently invoke kindness. Remind yourself you have a choice: you can ignore your suffering or punish yourself for your suffering—or you can give yourself a little hug, hold your own hand, and listen deeply to what you need.

Say, "May I give myself the compassion I need."

If a friend told you she was suffering for any reason—from a scratch to humiliation to a broken heart—you would be compassionate. You wouldn't snap at her, you wouldn't tell her to forget it, and you certainly wouldn't ignore her altogether. Why?

Because you love her, and because you know none of those things would help her. In fact, they would make her suffer even more. The same is true for you. Can you offer compassion to yourself in the same way you would offer it to your friend? Of course you can. Try it right now. See?

· · · · · · · · · ·

As you continue along your path of learning to love yourself, remember this affirmation. Perhaps fine-tune it to make it your own, or work with it exactly as it's written. Post it somewhere you will see it often, place it on your self-love altar, or write it inside the front cover of your notebook. Whenever you notice suffering of any kind arise within you, place one hand on your heart and one hand on your belly and repeat the affirmation as described above.

For way too many decades, I was obsessed with my weight and appearance. While I wasn't necessarily miserable over it every second of every day, the obsession was almost always lurking there in the background and casting a shadow over my joy. Like everyone in this culture, I received messages about the all-importance of appearance on an endless, repetitive loop. As a competitive gymnast, I remember restricting food as early as the age of eleven. And as an acting student right out of high school, I learned that I had to put my weight directly onto my resume and then staple it to my headshot to determine what type of roles I could get. I thought, *If I'm not thin enough, I won't be successful. If I'm not youthful enough, I won't be loved. If I'm not radiant or stylish or (whatever) enough, I should feel ashamed.* It went on like this for so long, it became like background noise, and I didn't realize just how much it was holding me back.

And it *was* holding me back. Even after I grew up and stopped trying to be the next big thing in gymnastics or the entertainment business, I still criticized and micromanaged my appearance pretty much every chance I got. I woke up, checked my body's shape in the mirror, and stepped immediately onto the scale. I restricted sugar, I restricted calories, and I drank way too much carbonated water and unsweetened herbal tea. And then I went to bed and vowed I would eat even "better" the following day. Even though I wasn't visibly emaciated, there were moments when my self-inflicted hunger was so intense, I would get dizzy when I stood up, and thoughts of food (eating it or not eating it) took up way too much real estate in my mind.

Now that I've acknowledged this soul-sucking pattern, it seems so obvious that a number on a scale is never worth throwing away my joy. But it took some doing to get here. One of the main obstacles was the message we hear over and over about how great it is to diet; how *empowered* we are when we ignore our bodies' messages and restrict calories or carbohydrates.

Lucky for me, I discovered the anti-diet/intuitive eating movement, which teaches that it's that very mindset of dieting that fuels disordered eating of all varieties—not just restrictive eating habits, but also binging habits—and the belief that if we let ourselves eat something, we'll never stop. In reality, none of this is true. When I first made the decision to stop restricting foods, I ate so much chocolate it was ridiculous. It was chocolate for every meal for a while! Then, once my body began to believe and trust that I was going to let myself eat the foods I was craving and to eat when I was hungry, I began to crave what my body needed, in an amount that was comfortable for me to consume. I never expected it would work this way! My mind was so certain it couldn't trust my body, and my body certainly had plenty of reasons not to trust my mind. It turns out that your body *does* know what it needs, after all. (There'll be lots more about intuitive eating in chapter 9.)

Of course, once my body got up to the weight that it wanted to be, I came face-to-face with the lack of self-love that had fueled my restrictive eating habits in the first place. It turned out the weight and appearance obsession was masking something deeper: a belief that my value as a person is questionable. Holding this belief, I realized, really hurts. When I examined this pain, I remembered being in high school and feeling like there were lots of valuable things about me other than my appearance, like my intelligence, my sense of humor, and just my status as a human being. Then, as I absorbed more and more cultural messages, I started to believe the world at large expected me to be pretty and sexy and didn't particularly care about anything else. Little by little, as I continued to approach adulthood and even into my early twenties, I moved further and further from a well-rounded self-image and closer and closer to a shameful sense that my body and sexuality were pretty much it: my only tickets to being admired, desired, and loved.

When I was twenty-one and already feeling pretty shaky about being on display as a female in the world, the story broke that President Bill Clinton had had an affair with White House aide Monica Lewinsky. The media, and pretty much everyone else, proceeded to viciously shame twenty-five-year-old Monica Lewinsky for her weight, her style, her behavior, and everything else she had the audacity to do or be. It was a classic case of damned if you do, damned if you don't. Even though the other person involved was twenty-seven years older than she was and quite literally *the most powerful person in the world*, there were zero voices defending Monica Lewinsky, at least that I heard.

Even so-called feminist leaders came out against her. While the cultural response to the situation was obviously a symptom of a bigger problem, the implication was loud and clear: young women everywhere should be fundamentally ashamed of themselves, whether they are too sexy or not sexy enough.

I don't mean to imply that I consciously realized this message at the time. If I had, I may have had a fighting chance at refuting it. Instead, I just internalized it, like, "I guess this is the real world. I guess I should try to avoid a similar fate. I guess I should learn how to be sexy enough not to be shamed for my lack of sexiness, but not so overtly sexual that I will be shamed for my sexuality. Whatever that means." Cue intense and seemingly inescapable shame.

Unfortunately, while the details may be different, this story is all too common. Even if you don't believe your worth is related to your appearance or sexuality, it's possible that you believe it's tied up in your degree of intelligence, or affluence, or success. We live in a culture that is structured around buying and selling things. This can warp our minds until we see *ourselves* as products. And so we attempt to conceptualize and gain control over our "worth" with questions like: *How valuable am I by the standards of the world? What do I have to offer? Am I a luxury item or an economy one? How can I increase my value as a product so I can be loved?*

In her liberating book *Beyond Beautiful,* author Anuschka Rees suggests naming and assigning a persona to the voice that criticizes your appearance. But if your most vocal inner critic fixates on something other than your appearance, it will still be helpful to name and conceptualize the voice. I see my inner body shamer as a sort of rapey party dude named Chad. Once I put a face and name to the voice, I realized Chad definitely wasn't me! *I* would never sling such horrible slurs! I am happy to report that

Chad lost a lot of power after that. Once I began picturing Chad as the source of the negative self-talk in my head, the negative self-talk started to taper off. It was like, *Hey, I get to choose my own thoughts and opinions! Why should I constantly be living in fear of what douchebag Chad will say? Beat it, lame ass.* (Luckily, I don't have to think about Chad any more. He was useful for a time, but once he was sufficiently demoted from a position of power in my mind, he sort of progressively dissolved back into the nothingness that was his original state.)

Your turn: take a moment to listen to the phrasing and tone of the voice that criticizes you mercilessly. If it were a person, what would it look like? What would be an appropriate name to give it?

The next time you notice this nasty inner voice piping up, remember it isn't you. *You* don't talk that way to anyone, or even *think* that way about anyone! Give the voice a withering look in your mind's eye as you realize just how crappy it really is. Tell it to get lost. Then maybe finish off with a round of the self-kindness affirmation as described above.

Be your own friend. Have compassion with yourself. Then say what you would say to a friend: *You are beautiful and valuable in so many ways and on so many levels. You are precious to me. You are perfect in my eyes. You are always doing the best you can, and that is plenty. You are enough, exactly as you are. I love you.*

Remember: this is a habit. Sure, your inner critic will still hurl some mean stuff at you from time to time. But the more you practice being kind to yourself, the more this will taper off. Like any habit, over time, being kind to yourself will become easier and easier and more and more natural.

Action Step
• KINDNESS ALARM •

If you want to be proactive about getting into the habit of being kind to yourself, for the next seven days, set an alert on your phone to notify you every hour throughout the day. Whenever it goes off, place one hand on your heart and one hand on your belly. Take some deep breaths and tune into yourself. Send yourself love and notice if you are berating yourself or criticizing yourself in any way. If you are, lovingly shift your monologue to a kinder one. Also, notice if there's anything you could use in order to feel better: a quick step outside for some fresh air, a muffin, a cup of tea, or a few minutes to listen to a favorite song through headphones.

Action Step
• SELF-CARE AUDIT •

Self-care is another wonderful way to be kind to yourself. Now would be a good time to assess ways you can deepen your self-care practice as you move through the remainder of this book. Grab your notebook and write down everything you can think of in this area. For example, is your sock or pajama drawer in need of some replenishment? Maybe an Epsom salt bath once a week will calm your anxiety and help you feel more grounded. Put it in your calendar! If you love to bake cookies, have you baked a batch lately? Or perhaps you will feel delightfully supported by a fridge stocked with fresh fruits and vegetables. Don't hold back: think of every self-care practice that might benefit you right now and then write it down. In the weeks and months ahead, keep an eye on this list and take action on it as you feel guided.

. . . .

To go back to my relationship with the Monica Lewinsky saga, now I am aware that there is another way to frame the story, and to frame my story about myself. I can look at myself as inherently valuable, worthy, and perfectly entitled to own and wield my own sexuality and personal power as I choose. I may not always look at myself that way, but simply knowing I don't have to subscribe to the mainstream cultural perspective that initially caused so much pain makes all the difference. I'm older now, but twenty-one-year-old me is still in there somewhere, and she feels much better now that I've taken the time to acknowledge and heal her suffering and to rewrite the narrative that caused it in the first place.

In the following exercise, you'll rewrite some old narratives of your own.

Action Step
• REWRITE YOUR STORIES •

In a journal or notebook, brainstorm all the stories you can think of that may be holding you back. Then, tell yourself new ones that you like better, with proof or a real-life example that the old story doesn't have to be true for you. Here are some examples, starting with mine from above:

Old story: I can only be valued if I am a desirable sex object.

New story: Everyone is a multi-faceted being. We are valuable for so much more than just our sexuality and appearance.

Proof: Monica Lewinsky's activism and advocacy in recent years. Greta Thunberg. Tina Fey. Oprah Winfrey. Louise Hay.

Old story: I have to be successful at my career in order to be valuable.

New story: I am inherently valuable.

Proof: My younger brother. While he is quite successful, I have seen the same amount of (immense!) value in him throughout his life, even before he was successful in the eyes of the world. In fact, I feel this exact same way about everyone I love. I can feel this way about myself too.

Old story: I should be further along in my career by now. It's too late to try anything new.

New story: You don't have to in order to be valuable, but if you want to, you can reinvent yourself and kickstart a satisfying career at any age.

Proof: Baddiewinkle (look her up on Instagram) became a unique and wildly popular social media influencer while in her eighties. Charles Darwin didn't become well-known until he published *On the Origin of Species* when he was fifty. Laura Ingalls Wilder didn't publish her first book until she was sixty-five.

On the other hand, if you have weak knees or a shattered hip and you want to be an Olympic skier, you may want to revisit that desire. Perhaps the story that needs to change in such a case is not the story that you can't do it, but rather the idea that you need to be an Olympic skier in order to be happy.

Ultimately, whatever the limiting story is, if it's limiting you, there is always a new story you can tell. Whether it's, "I'm stuck in this relationship," "I'm stuck in this job," "No one from my hometown could ever make it big," "The only thing that will make me happy is being an Olympic skier," or *anything* else, I don't want you saying, "Well, okay, but *this one's* true." I want you to look honestly at that story and switch it to something that frees you. You can only be free when the stories you tell yourself are stories that support your freedom, your power, and your joy.

Nothing could be kinder than opening a cage and setting something free. Be kind to yourself. Set yourself free.

Four
LET'S FORGET ABOUT BEING AWESOME

You are awesome in a lot of ways. But you are definitely not awesome in *every* way … because nobody is.

There has been a lot of emphasis on self-esteem in recent decades. *Esteem* means holding a high opinion. *Self-esteem* means holding a high opinion of yourself: of your strengths, talents, abilities, and appearance. Self-esteem has nothing to do with self-love. Self-esteem is not a superpower. It's just an opinion.

Self-esteem in and of itself is not *bad*. It's fine! But thinking that you have to have a high opinion of yourself *in every life area* is an impossible standard. Impossible standards result in delusion or disappointment, both of which can lead to depression. That's why it's wonderfully freeing to give up on self-esteem entirely. Don't worry about it. Don't try and cultivate it. Don't feel guilty or flawed for not having more of it. Just let it go.

To clarify, self-esteem is thinking, "My body is so sexy. It should be on the cover of a magazine." Self-love is thinking, "My body works so hard every day pumping my blood and digesting my food and carrying me from place to place. It's so loyal and it's always doing its best. I treasure it and feel grateful for it no matter what it looks like. And even if I think negative thoughts about it sometimes, I know that's normal and I don't beat myself up for beating myself up. I just notice the negative thought and then do my best to let it go."

Self-esteem is thinking, "I am super smart. I am probably the smartest person in this room." Self-love is thinking, "I have no idea how smart I am compared to the other people in this room because there's no way of knowing. And honestly, it doesn't matter anyway." Or even, "I love being around highly intelligent people because they always have something interesting to teach me. And even if I feel inadequate for a second, I don't let that depress me or keep me from enjoying connecting with people because I know everyone feels that way sometimes."

The pressure to have self-esteem can actually *undermine* our self-esteem. The reality is that no one can (or should) be awesome at everything.

It's not just that you don't have to be awesome in every way in order to be worthy of love and approval. It's that you don't have to be awesome in *any* way to be worthy of love and approval. Think about it: who is someone you really love? Consider your son, your daughter, your cat, your dog, your brother, your sister, your mom, your dad, your partner, or your best friend. Bring to mind someone you just absolutely adore.

Why do you love and adore this person or animal? Because they're a world-class skateboarder? Because they're the best driver on the road? Because they look like a swimsuit model? Because they're the most popular cat on Instagram? Nope. In fact, when you really and truly love someone, you desperately wish they could know they never have to be any of those things. You want them to see themselves through your eyes because your eyes see them as they really are: inherently worthy of love no matter how epic or excellent or exceptional they are or are not in the eyes of the world.

I'm not saying we should all just give up and be lazy and never accomplish anything or improve ourselves. What I *am* saying is that you don't need to accomplish or improve in order to establish your worth or increase your *esteem* in your own eyes or the eyes of the world. You can do it because it feels fun and joyful and expansive, or because you just sort of feel like it.

So give up on being super spiritual and having the best meditation habits. Give up on eating nothing but health food and becoming the next Miss America. Of course, do those things if you want to! But stop making them a prerequisite to self-worth. You don't have to master anything or be the best at anything, but if you do, do it out of a sincere enthusiasm rather than a belief that you have to excel in some (or every) way in order to be lovable. You're lovable now. You were born lovable. You'll never be any more or less lovable.

I read an article recently in *Mindful* magazine about people who spend a lot of time around death and dying. In it, I came across this quote from author Rabbi Rami Shapiro, which I love: "I would push back on the notion that your life has to amount to something. It's just an amazing thing that you exist at all."[4] Indeed, when you imagine looking back at your life from your

4. Stephanie Domet, "Living Greatly," *Mindful*, December 2019, 52–63.

deathbed, do you think you will wish you had been more impressive in the eyes of the world? I don't. I think I will wish I had been less distracted by being impressive at all. I think I will wish I had just gone swimming instead of worrying about what I looked like in a swimsuit. I think I will wish I had enjoyed the process of writing instead of worrying about whether or not people would approve of what I wrote. I think I will wish I had devoted the entirety of my attention to wonderment, enjoyment, and awe—not to worrying whether or not I was good enough in some way but soaking in the miracle of being here at all.

The fact is that while most of us excel at a handful of things, we are also mediocre at a lot more things and really terrible at everything else. That is *a fact*. And so what?

For a moment, imagine meeting someone who is awesome at everything and in every way. First of all, let's be honest: you probably wouldn't like this person. Because who could relate? And what a bore! And second of all, they wouldn't really be *all* that awesome. They couldn't! Because there is no one on Earth who is. So this is a completely implausible scenario. It's likelier you'll meet Bigfoot.

A number of times in the past when I've taught or attended a spiritual workshop at a larger event or venue, such as a conference or retreat center, I've felt inadequate upon arrival, like someone who vaguely but fundamentally didn't belong. The other people at the venue seemed somehow wiser, cooler, richer, or more glamorous, and I felt like they all knew each other and maybe even had inside jokes together. This made me feel both ashamed and resentful. But luckily, I've learned to remind myself at times like these that my feelings of inadequacy aren't based in reality and the comparisons I'm making aren't actually relevant to anything. And that pretty much everyone else is almost certainly feeling the very same way and thinking the very same things about themselves.

That's why when I teach, I often like to start off my workshops by naming this feeling. I ask if anyone else feels like I do when they first arrive, like they are the odd man out, and somehow not as wonderful as the other people in the workshop, or at the venue in general. When I say this, the whole room nods. You can feel the group loosen up with laughter and quiet sighs of relief. It's amazing how much everyone lets down their guard once we get the illusion of personal inadequacy out in the open and see it for what it is: a trick of the mind.

I find it helpful to constantly remind myself of this at parties where I don't know many people. My initial instinct is that no one will want to talk to me because they will all have better things to do and more interesting people to talk to. But then I override that thought by reminding myself: those partygoers quietly sipping their drinks feel just as fundamentally deficient as I do. On some level, everyone feels lonely, bashful, and insecure. Even people who seem to exude confidence are shy and worried underneath it all, sometimes even more so than the ones who are obviously introverted. And often a feeling of inadequacy can come across as prickliness or standoffishness or even superiority. Ultimately, there's not a person on Earth who doesn't want to be seen, heard, and appreciated for who they are. Armed with this inner reminder, any party can become a delight as you connect with that spark of magic behind someone's eyes while asking them where they come from and what they care about. It's amazing how a person blossoms before you when you bust through the initial fear and bathe them in the insecurity-melting sunlight of your interest and attention.

As an antidote to stage fright, I once heard someone say, "Bless, don't impress." This is a useful motto for all situations. Wherever you go and whatever you do, go around blessing instead of impressing. Bless yourself and others with love instead of trying to impress yourself or others with your fabulousness. It's such a load off and it makes life so much more fun.

In the tarot, the first card is not number one. There's a card before that: zero. Tarot card number zero is called the Fool. The Fool is traditionally portrayed as a happy-go-lucky sort of fellow setting out on a journey, with all of his earthly belongings tied in a small bundle on a stick slung over his shoulder. Along with a scrappy little dog, he is exuberantly sauntering along a cliff, perilously close to the edge. Like the number zero itself, the Fool exemplifies the power of emptiness: of being free of stories and expectations, and completely open to whatever life brings. He not only doesn't need to be the best at something, he doesn't need to have any mastery over anything at all. And this is the ultimate mastery. Because without this energy within us, we would never try anything new or do anything that involved the unexpected. We couldn't learn anything because we would need to be great at it from the very first try. Clearly, if we aren't willing to play the Fool—to be amateurish, imprudent, or even spectacularly awkward and naive—life will be predictable, boring, and basically the worst.

Everything contains its opposite: there is no one who excels at something who is not extremely familiar with the path of the Fool. Who is your favorite musician? Rest assured they have made far more terrible songs than good ones. Is there someone you admire for their uncommon and adventurous life? They could never have lived it without setting out on countless paths they'd never been down before and had no idea how to navigate.

When you give up on being awesome at everything—when you get comfortable with being an absolute zero—a whole world of possibility opens up to you because you are open to everything. Right away, you begin to reap the joy of this life experience, and you realize that life is not about achieving awesomeness or being a badass. It's about every step of the journey, including the step that is, even now, beneath your feet. It's a trick of the ego to think you have to arrive on some special scene and electrify everyone you meet in order to start living a life that matters. The life that matters is already here. It's within you and all around you. It's *now*.

Moving forward, instead of holding up an index finger to tell the world we're a number one, let's hold one hand in the shape of a circle and proudly declare that we are a zero: free, open, empty, and inherently worthy with or without the perception of awesomeness in the eyes of the world. Like, *Look, ma! I'm a zero! I'm choosing to need nothing, expect nothing, and even be nothing. And so I am open to everything.* How liberating is that?

Action Step
• HONESTLY ASSESS •

In a journal or notebook, without thinking too much and without judging yourself, quickly list:

- Five ways you are awesome in the eyes of the world. (Examples: you have a nice car, your hair is luxurious, you teach packed yoga classes, your wardrobe is spectacular, your teeth are gleaming)

- Five ways you are *not* awesome in the eyes of the world. (Examples: you have no car, your hair is thinning, no one goes to your yoga classes, you're not too fashionable, your teeth are stained and chipped)

- Five things you are currently great at. (Examples: typing, lifting weights, parallel parking, making friends, baking muffins)

- Five things you are not currently great at. (Examples: algebra, singing, nail art, wearing scarves, making pizza dough)

- Five things you have no idea whether or not you will be good at, but that you definitely want to try anyway. (Examples: stand-up comedy, backpacking, goat yoga, playing the drums, growing tomatoes)

Remember: none of this has any bearing on your worth, or on your right to enjoy your life in this moment. We all have things we're great at, not so great at, and terrible at. And these things can fluctuate! For example, while I'm fairly sure at this point I'll never be able to carry a tune, one of these days I might very well figure out how to make delicious pizza dough. And when I remember that I don't have to be the next Charlie Watts, learning to play the drums sounds like a blast. My point is, let's give up on awesome. Let's follow the example of the Fool. Let's let go of the need to be number one, and step into the immediate, vast, astonishing power of zero.

Before we move on to chapter 5, it's time for an energetic reset with the next action step.

Action Step
• CLEAR, CLEAN, AND CLEANSE •

To symbolize your glorious release of the need to be awesome or to prove your worth in the eyes of the world, go through your stuff and let go of anything you don't love, use, or need. If an article of clothing doesn't fit you right or doesn't help you feel comfortable in your own skin, donate it to a thrift store. If the flavorless protein bars in your cupboard are only there out of the hope that you can change your body into something it doesn't naturally want to be, throw them in a grocery bag and haul them to a food bank. If your bathroom scale has no earthly purpose other than to measure your worth through the lens of your body weight (and chances are good that it doesn't), find a new home for it. If a painting on your wall depicts something that doesn't nourish your soul, get it out of your world.

In general, this is the perfect time to get rid of absolutely anything that's been cluttering up your space. Go through your wallet and let go of old receipts. Delete old downloads from your computer and old photos from your phone. Organize your sock drawer. Get rid of unfinished projects that you honestly don't feel excited about finishing. If something is broken and you're not willing or able to fix it, say goodbye. Be thorough: if you've been renting a storage space, go through it and ask yourself if you actually need the stuff that's already been demoted to a space outside of your home. Also remember your car, your workspace, and anywhere else you've stashed physical stuff.

When you take the time to do this, you'll soon realize that this is no paltry or mundane act. The inner shifts that occur when you let go of clutter from your outer world are immense. And when you pair your clutter-clearing efforts with the clear intention to let go of the desperate need to be awesome, you will slowly but surely begin to feel nondesperately awesome: awesome in an authentic way, rather than in a way that is constantly seeking approval in the eyes of the world.

Don't feel a rush to move on to the next chapter. Just let yourself get carried away with the clutter-clearing process and continue with it until it feels complete. Next, clean! Give your space a thorough physical cleaning. Finally, bless your space with an energy clearing. Here are some general guidelines for clearing the energy in your home:

- First, make noise. Find a drum or a rattle, or just grab a pot and a wooden spoon. Move around each room and area of your home while making noise with your chosen noisemaker. (If you have pets, you may want to do this when they are not in the room so as not to frighten them.)

- Next, cleanse the space with sage or incense smoke or an aromatherapy spray (again, be sure to do this when your pets are elsewhere). If you're burning incense or a bundle of sage, carry a dish or a plate to catch any burning embers. Again, move methodically through each room or area.

- Fine-tune the energy. This time, move through each room and area as you ring a beautiful chime or bell, or simply chant "Om."

- Finally, stand near your self-love altar or in another location in your home that feels right. Place your palms together in prayer pose, close your eyes, and take some

deep breaths to calm and center your mind. Imagine
a sphere of golden-white light completely filling and
encompassing your entire home. See it gently spinning
in a clockwise direction to seal in the positive energy.
Call on the Divine in a way that feels powerful for you,
and request and envision positive energies swirling in
and around your home: energies that support your newly
burgeoning and expanding self-love. Feel and express
gratitude as you say or think, "Thank you, thank you,
thank you. Blessed be. And so it is."

Five
COMPLIMENTS ARE COMPLICATED

I know something about you: you love compliments. Granted, you may be weird about them! Perhaps they make you feel awkward or blushy or like you don't know how to respond. But simply by virtue of the fact that you are a human being, I am 100 percent certain that on some level, in a very real way, you love it when someone says something nice about you. So do I! So does everybody.

We are a social species. We want to be liked and desired and approved of. It's how we're built.

The problem is that compliments can give us such a rush of euphoric brain chemicals, we can get carried away with chasing them and living for them and dreading the day when they stop coming our way. We can begin to give other peoples' opinions of us more power in our lives than our own comfort, inspiration, and joy. And that's no way to live.

When I learned about the antidiet movement and it finally dawned on me that I was eating way less food than my body actually wanted and needed in order to be comfortable and healthy, I was forced to face my lifelong fear of putting on weight. While I was slowly but surely allowing my body to discover its more natural size and shape, I went through many ups and downs. Sometimes I was ecstatic, and sometimes I was despondent. Sometimes I was glowing with pride, and other times I was crying and cowering in shame.

One thing I thought about a lot in the early days of eating enough food was how much I relished compliments about my teeny tiny body and how sad I was to have to let those go. But ultimately, I realized that while compliments are nice to receive, they aren't *that* nice. They're not so nice that I should sacrifice my comfort, my health, and my inner peace in order to get them. And anyway, wouldn't it be nicer to receive compliments about how radiant and happy and healthy I appear—or even better: how funny or insightful or kind I am—rather than compliments about how little pressure I exert on a scale?

Sometimes, I like to imagine myself all alone in a cottage in the middle of the woods, living my whole life among trees and flowers and animals, without another human being in sight. In such a situation (I ask myself), would I restrict food so I could remain unnaturally tiny? Would I freak out about a bad hair day? Would I try to fit in to the latest fashion even if I felt more comfortable in my supposedly outdated pair of thrift store jeans? Would I compare myself to the supermodel du jour or the British royal family or *Vanity Fair's* movers and shakers lists and decide I didn't measure up? Nope. Never. Not even a little bit. And neither would you. Why? Because there would be no compliments to seek or criticisms to dodge: no one would have an opinion of you that you would feel you needed to control. So you would just be content with being you.

Only... you wouldn't. As the only human in your world, it wouldn't be long before you would get lonely. Humans like being around other humans. Some of us like being around other humans often, and others not as often, but all of us like to be around them sometimes. And we like them to like us: to admire us, approve of us, and (on occasion) desire us. This is not a choice: this is evolution. For the very survival of our species (whether or not these are conscious goals of ours) we evolved to crave inclusive support from our tribe and to seek positive attention from potential sexual partners.

So we can see why compliments (and likes on social media for that matter) flood our brains with feel-good chemicals. But to take it a step further, we can also look deeply and see that *chasing* compliments—and, by the same token, trying to avoid criticism—can cause us to live in fear and desperation, which floods our brains with feel-*bad* chemicals. When desperation for approval becomes a way of life, the hits of good feelings from compliments become like tiny lines of cocaine smuggled into a dark prison cell. In other words, compliment addiction can lead to the saddest and emptiest of lives.

It's amazing how clearly I can recall compliments and criticisms of all varieties, even from a very early age. I'm willing to bet you're the same way. It's as if we are all so confused about who we are and so in the dark about how we are seen, we are desperate for any shred of a clue to how we are seen in the world, no matter whether it was uttered with rudeness or helpfulness, envy or genuine admiration. Here's just a small sampling of the opinions I remember others expressing about me:

- When I was nine, a boy in my fourth-grade class said, "You know why I don't like you? Because your hands and feet are really small compared to your body." This freaked me out for years. After he said that, I imagined everyone was quietly judging my tiny feet and hands when they saw me. Now, I realize the opinion was almost certainly unique to the boy, and I also realize that even if my feet and hands *had* been exceptionally small compared to my body, it needn't have mattered one bit.

- As a freshman in high school, a couple of guys walked by me and I heard one of them make a comment about my breasts that I don't need to repeat, but suffice it to say I remember it verbatim.

- Speaking of unsolicited comments about my breasts, within the last few years, I posted a video on my YouTube channel about the ancient holiday of Beltane, and it was shared somewhat widely. Many of the comments were kind and encouraging, but the one I remember the most was from a man who typed, simply, "You need to grow some boobs." While this would have devastated me when I was younger, now I felt more bent out of shape on behalf of women in general, rather than on my own behalf.

- At a party last year, a good friend of mine told me that every time she looked at me, I was deep in conversation with someone. She said I had a knack for listening deeply to people, and that I made them feel seen. That was one of the best compliments I've ever received. I will treasure it always.

When I assess the comments and criticisms I've received over the years, one of the takeaways for me is that comments about appearance are especially problematic. While, "I love that coat," or "You look radiant," are obviously not terrible, I personally would prefer if we all just agreed not to talk about appearance at all. Or, if we do talk about appearance, I wish we could talk about something eternal such as the color of someone's eyes or the contagious nature of their smile. There's just so much baggage around appearance in our culture that I wish we could universally exclude it from possible conversation topics. There is a similar amount of cultural baggage (and potential for cattiness, envy, and hidden agendas) connected to compliments related to wealth, status, or success.

Of course, we can't control what others say, and it would be exhausting to silently judge everyone who innocently makes an appearance or status-related comment. But what we *can* do is personally vow to go beyond the surface level of things when we connect with others. We can, like my dear friend at the party, look past appearances and external measures of success and into what *truly* makes someone fabulous; for example, their personality, their unique way of looking at things, their ability to be fully present, and their capacity to love.

What's more, we can personally free ourselves from the mental prison of obsessive approval-seeking/disapproval-dodging. We can vow to enjoy compliments, rise above the subtle drama of envy, and even dodge the downward spiral that disapproval may have instigated in the past. In short, we can stop being a slave to the thoughts and opinions of others. How, exactly, do we do this? The answer lies in voluntary vulnerability. In *The Gifts of Imperfection*, author and researcher Brené Brown writes, "Imperfections are not inadequacies; they are reminders that we are all in this together."[5] When you allow your insecurity to be what it is without trying to avoid it or numb it or override it with a flood of approval, you will discover *more* connection with others—not less—because we *all* feel insecure, and vulnerable, and afraid we'll be ostracized by the tribe or rejected by potential romantic partners.

But approval-seeking is like a world full of insecure people trying to appear to be Superman or Wonder Woman all the time. It's a really lonely world to live in. While we may feel temporarily euphoric when someone compliments us on our ability to leap buildings in a single bound, we'll never feel the genuine human connection that we actually crave.

Brené Brown also wrote, "What's the greater risk? Letting go of what other people think or letting go of how I feel, what I believe, and who I am?"[6] Without how we feel, what we believe, and who we are, we can never feel seen, known, and truly loved. Yes, compliments are nice, but real connection is better. We can have both, but only if we value our real selves—insecurities, challenges, and all—more than we value convincing the world of our superhuman strength, status, or superiority.

None of us is actually Superman. And being Superman would be lonely anyway. So let's love and accept ourselves exactly as we are instead. That's the real superpower, because it opens us up to the fullness of this human experience: to the tender truth of who we are and the tender truth of who *everyone* is. We are all these adorable little jewel-eyed creatures who have no idea what is going on here and who are all doing our best and trying to make friends and find comfort and inspiration and love on this

---

5. Brené Brown, *The Gifts of Imperfection: Let Go of Who You Think You're Supposed to Be and Embrace Who You Are*, (Center City, MN: Hazelden, 2010), 61.
6. Ibid., 125.

tiny planet, spiraling with other tiny planets around one of billions of tiny little stars.

So let's just be that.

And when we compliment other people, let's compliment them for real things that actually matter, such as how wise they are, or how much they've been through, or how their eyes sparkle with laughter, or how they exude an aura of peace. Let it come from your heart: from a feeling of love, whether you've known them forever or you are just passing them briefly in this life as they ring up your groceries or sit next to you on a bus. "You seem like an artist to me—are you?" "You have the best laugh." "You really listen when I talk."

It will also benefit us to be awake to the motivations behind compliments: whether we're giving or receiving them. For example, not long after I published my first book, I presented a workshop at a popular convention, and the room was pretty packed. After the talk, a lot of people came up to meet me or to have me sign their books. Even though I'd say I did pretty well for one of my first workshops, I still naturally felt vulnerable. Of course I did! I still feel vulnerable when I present workshops, but at that time it was all new to me, and I was learning as I went. I was moving out of my comfort zone in a pretty serious way. While a number of other people stood around listening, a man about my age, whom I had never met, looked me in the eye and said something like, "You have a lot of interesting material to share." He could have stopped there, but instead he went on. "You could definitely embody your power more when you are in front of a group," he said. "You need to ground your energy and take more deep breaths while you speak." Instantly, I felt the wind rush out of my sails. My budding sense of accomplishment turned to shame. In the moment, I assumed he must be right, and that everyone must have been thinking the same thing. Later, when I told a cousin of mine about this exchange (she spent many years touring as a punk vocalist in an overwhelmingly male world), she pointed out that this man was not trying to help me, but to tear me down in order to assuage his own feelings of inadequacy. After that incident, I experienced many similarly "helpful" men who had something to say to me after a workshop. Luckily, moving forward, I was prepared for those men. I was able to recognize their underlying motivations and not let their comments crush me like that first one did.

Compliments—even without criticisms tacked on to the end—can also be catty. If someone is jealous of you, for example, they may "compliment" you in a way that you can tell is not generous. Even if the words themselves are inarguably complimentary, like, "I love your outfit. You always look so put-together," you can sometimes sense the unspoken subtext to be something like, "I feel like such a slob around you. Do you have to make the rest of us feel so inadequate?" So-called compliments like these leave you feeling less connected to the other person, rather than more.

Simply being conscious of the less-than-straightforward nature of these sorts of loaded or backhanded compliments is the most important step in not getting pulled into their negative undercurrents. That way, we become empowered to rise above the boomerang of negativity and instead choose to direct compassion toward this person who is clearly feeling insecure.

This light of awareness can also help you to recognize any untoward motivations in your comments toward others. That way, before you express a catty or uncomplimentary "compliment," or a compliment that emphasizes your feelings of insecurity rather than your genuine admiration, you can recognize your own feelings of insecurity and send love and compassion to yourself. Because ultimately, making other people feel worse—or even pointing out that we feel inferior to them—is never going to make us feel better, at least not in any real and lasting sense.

Now, it's time to assess the compliments and criticisms that have affected you over the years. We all have them. So grab your notebook or journal.

Action Step
• COMPLIMENT AND CRITICISM AUDIT •

First, brainstorm every compliment that stands out in your mind from childhood onward. Next, brainstorm every criticism that had a big effect on you. Then, brainstorm the gray areas, such as compliments that were not really compliments, or that were actually criticisms in disguise.

When you've written out everything you can think of, put down your pen and take a moment with each item. Consider how this comment made you feel, and how much you took it to heart. Did it shape your behavior? Did it add to or diminish your joy? Did it color the way you thought of yourself for years to come? Think about the motive of whoever said it: is it possible it came from a place of fear, or worry, or insecurity? If the comment had a negative effect on you, can you go deeply into the origin of the comment and see that it was never actually about you? If it had a wholly positive effect on you, can you see how it (very likely) came from someone who was speaking from love rather than fear, abundance rather than lack?

Next, I'd like for you to make a list of compliments that would truly nourish you in a deep and genuine way. What would you most like people to think about you? What would you most like to think about yourself? See if you can go beyond the ego desires for compliments about how stylish or rich or talented you are and connect with your soul's truest desires to be authentically seen and appreciated. For example:

> I love being around you.
> Your joy is contagious.
> Your generosity of spirit inspires me.
> Your laugh is like music.
> You have a talent for seeing the best in people.
> You are so brave!
> I love how you are always trying new things.

See if you can write a whole page of such statements. Don't worry about whether or not you think you deserve these compliments. Just write out anything you would love to be true about you. Once you've written a whole page, change the compliments into affirmations. So, to use the above compliments as examples, you could change them to:

> Other people love being around me.
> My joy is contagious.
> My generosity of spirit inspires others.
> My laugh is like music.
> I have a talent for seeing the best in people.
> I am so brave! I am always trying new things.

While you may not believe me quite yet, these things are all true about you. As long as you faithfully followed the above direction to override your ego and connect with your soul's truth, there is not a single statement on your list that does not describe you to a T.

Follow-Up Action Step
• AFFIRM WHAT'S ALREADY TRUE •

For the next seven days, read the list of affirmations you just composed aloud to yourself last thing before bed and first thing in the morning. As you do this, put as much belief and conviction into your voice as you possibly can, even if it makes you feel super awkward and self-conscious at first.

Follow-Up Action Step
• GIVE REAL COMPLIMENTS •

To internalize this wisdom even further, when you interact with others this week, see if you can go beyond their self-consciousness or ego-related behavior and tap into their authentic, divine selves. Give at least two compliments to other people daily and offer compliments that foster greater connection rather than divisiveness. In other words, be generous and speak to the true, eternal self of the other. Even if you're just saying, "I love the color of your eyes," the important thing is the energy and intention behind the compliment more than the content of the compliment. Speak to their eternal beauty rather than their fleeting beauty. Remember that the greatness of others in no way diminishes your own and can only amplify it. Remember that what you focus on expands, and that when you focus on the Divine and transcendent nature of others, your own divine and transcendent nature cannot help but be amplified in turn.

Six
BOUNDARIES ARE BEAUTIFUL

"Setting healthy boundaries," sounds like something that would keep you insulated from human connection, like you are the proverbial rock on your own little insulated island of emotional safety. But healthy boundaries actually help you connect *more* with others, not less—and in a more nourishing and sustainable way. You know those truths that seem like contradictions when you first encounter them? This is one of those.

I grew up with pretty much no concept of boundaries. The summer before I started kindergarten, when I was four and a half, I began living in two houses rather than one. I stayed with my mom on weekdays and my dad—who lived about forty minutes away in the town we had all lived in together before the split—on weekends. During the summer, when school was out, the pattern was reversed.

While, in retrospect, I can see that I was absolutely devastated by having to move away from everything familiar and to have my one home split into two, my overriding thoughts, even as a very young girl, were about the well-being of my parents. I could sense that they were both sad, and I wanted to make them happy in any way I could. Unfortunately, my parents encouraged this. For example, I remember crying one night in my dark bedroom and my mother asking me what was wrong. Although even then I had a sense that it was the "wrong" thing to say, I tearfully told her the truth, which was, "I miss Daddy." In response, I don't remember the words she used, but I do remember that she snapped at me and left the room. Needless to say, her response caused me to feel even more pain. I quickly learned that it was best not to focus on my own challenging feelings and instead to do what I could to minimize hers.

When I got a little older, I sometimes wanted to stay in the town where my mom lived (and where I went to school) over the weekend so I could do something social with someone from school, like attend a birthday party or see a movie. When I would ask my dad if it was okay, he wouldn't say no, but he would in some way manage to communicate that he would be sad and lonely if I didn't visit him that weekend. Nothing was worse to me than the thought that I would cause my father pain. Soon, I stopped asking, which meant I very rarely got to spend time with my classmates outside of school.

The older I got, the more enmeshed I became in my parent's emotional well-being. By the age of eleven or twelve, I remember feeling like I was the only one who understood either of my parents and like they both needed me to be there to keep them from spiraling into loneliness and depression. While in a way this gave me a sense of inflated importance, it certainly didn't contribute to a carefree childhood. It also co-opted my sense of self: I saw myself as an emotional crutch for both of my parents, and not as my own sovereign being. In my mind, their emotional needs took so much precedence over my own that I didn't perceive myself as someone with emotional needs at all.

This untenable situation came to a head when I was thirteen. My dad had been systematically urging me to tell my mom I wanted to go to high school in his town (the town of my birth) rather than the town she had relocated us to after the divorce. This put me in a really difficult position because I knew my mom would be devastated if I did that, but I also could see that my dad would be devastated if I didn't. When I finally buckled to my dad's pressure and told my mom I wanted to change school districts, she predictably collapsed in tears. I then became so inconsolable that—to their credit—my parents collectively decided to put me in therapy. And that was when I had the astounding good fortune of meeting a counselor who would help me—for the first time ever—realize that it was okay and even preferable for me to check in with myself and speak up for myself before trying to take care of everyone else. As this counselor put it, "You don't need to be the czar of everyone's emotions." This was an absolute revelation. It's a statement that resounds within me to this day.

Of course, my home situations being what they were, speaking up for myself and my feelings very rarely went over well, so it was far from an overnight cure. But having *some* awareness of what I thought, felt, and needed was immeasurably better than having none at all. And the very concept of *not needing to be the czar of everyone's emotions* took up residence in my consciousness and acted as a compass, helping me eventually, as an adult, find my way to emotional independence.

Unsurprisingly, my first major romantic relationship after I left home at the age of eighteen was crushingly codependent. Merriam-Webster defines *codependency* as "a psychological condition or relationship in which a person is controlled or manipulated by another who is affected with a pathological condition (such as an addiction to alcohol or heroin)."[7] Indeed, this young partner of mine had recently ended an addiction to a heavy drug and was not in a good place psychologically by any stretch of the imagination. In my twisted world, this was heaven: someone who could transfer their dependence, easily and perfectly, directly from drugs to me.

Needless to say, it's been quite a road from there to where I am now. Of course, no two journeys are alike, so your situation is undoubtedly different than mine. Nevertheless, it's my sincere hope that by sharing what I've learned about boundaries, I can save you some of the heartache I experienced, and perhaps some of the long, difficult, and confusing years of trial and error—or at least help you feel less alone. No matter who you are or what type of background you came from, boundaries are an important key to loving yourself and reaping all the magical benefits that loving yourself provides.

First of all, in order to have healthy boundaries, you need to know what you are thinking and feeling. It sounds so simple, but when I think back to my adolescence and early adulthood, I can see that I had no true sense of what I wanted, needed, or preferred in any given situation. It never even occurred to me to take a moment to check in with myself. Instead, I was busy thinking of what everyone else thought of me: did they value me? Did

---

7. *Merriam-Webster,* "Codependency," July 2020, https://www.merriam-webster.com/dictionary/codependency.

they need me? Did they feel comforted when I was around? What could I do to help them feel better, and in the process, to get them to like me, love me, and approve of me?

Action Steps
• BREATHE AND WRITE •

There are many useful ways to check in with yourself and to cultivate a cherished relationship with yourself. Taking even just five minutes of alone time every day to breathe, relax, and listen to your body is a vital key. Your self-love altar would be the perfect place for this simple exercise. You might even consider placing a mirror above your altar so you can gaze lovingly into your own eyes while you do it. Another practical tool for the purpose is journaling. I like to freewrite three notebook pages every morning without stopping. This is an exercise recommended by Julia Cameron in her seminal self-help book *The Artist's Way*, and it's been an essential part of my self-care practice for years. While I write I often surprise myself to learn what I'm actually feeling. And then once I fill a notebook from cover to cover, I look back over what I've written and notice the overarching themes: what I've worried about, what I'm dreaming about, and generally what's been going on with me mentally, emotionally, and physically. Three pages is a lot for most people, so if you prefer to do two pages or even just one, that will be wonderful too.

· · · · · · · · · ·

Once you're more in tune with yourself, the next step is to *prioritize* yourself. From experience, I know that if you aren't used to the idea of prioritizing your own experience over the experience of others, the very idea will sound unforgivably selfish at first. You may even be tempted to reject it. If you are, stay with me for just another moment so I can illustrate what I'm actually talking about.

Imagine you're having lunch with a friend. While you're finishing up your meal, you get the idea that it would be nice to go for a walk around a nearby lake together afterward, so you suggest this to your friend. Unbeknownst to you, your friend has an important doctor's appointment within the next hour, and she won't be able to make the appointment if she goes for a walk around the lake with you. Would you want her to tell you about the appointment? Or would you prefer that she paste on a smile and agree while silently thinking, "I really need to get to that appointment, but it will hurt my friend's feelings if I don't go for a walk around the lake, so I guess I'll have to skip it.'"

Obviously, even if it caused you momentary disappointment, you would very much prefer the former—for so many reasons! By being honest with you about the appointment, she would not only get to take care of her health, she would also be connecting with you in a sincere way by letting you know her true thoughts and feelings. Because how would you guess? You couldn't. And when you know what she is really thinking and feeling, your relationship becomes more authentic. This is an example of how healthy boundaries help you connect more with people—not less.

Now, not everyone is as generous and as authentic as you are. Some people *would* want their friend to put on a happy face and go along with whatever they wanted to do. If you happen to be in a relationship with someone like this, your honesty about your thoughts and feelings will not go over well. But, ultimately, this is a good thing! Even if it's uncomfortable in the moment, it will reveal that your relationship is not a healthy one. If a relationship becomes too uncomfortable after you begin to speak your truth and to speak up for your needs, it will be a good idea to let go of that relationship to make room for a healthier and more equal one.

Of course, sometimes your truth won't be as straightforward as, "I can't because I have a doctor's appointment." Sometimes a date will ask you if you want to stay the night and you simply won't want to. Sometimes a dear friend will invite you out for drinks and you'll sincerely want to stay in and read a true crime novel in your pajamas. Sometimes your parents will want you to visit for the holidays and you'll realize you'd much prefer to visit literally any other time of the year. But even these truths are worthy of being spoken. (Not that you have to be blunt about it. For example, instead of, "I'd rather read a true crime novel than hang out with you," it would be just as true to say, "I really need to stay in and rest tonight but I'd love to take a rain check.") When you honor yourself and your desires first, you will actually be a better friend and family member because you'll be offering who you really are, and not who you think you should be.

About seven years ago, it came to my attention that my relationship with an elder female family member was not entirely honest. When I was an adolescent, this family member brought someone into my life who sexually abused me. And while I had mentioned this to her, we had never discussed it in depth. For the first time, I realized that I felt angry with her for allowing this abuser into my life and continuing to put me in his care. Because I hadn't been consciously aware of this anger, I hadn't dealt with it, and—as survivors of childhood abuse will do before they have consciously learned to do otherwise—I was internalizing it. In other words, I was directing it toward myself. I was harboring a belief that I had deserved the abuse because I was shameful and tainted in some fundamental but invisible way.

This was no small realization, and it certainly wasn't simple. Along with it came the realization that my relationship with this female family member was still woefully codependent. Though decades had come and gone, I was still prioritizing her feelings over my own. Because of this, I asked her if we could go together to talk to my childhood counselor, whom I had experienced success with years before.

At the appointment, the therapist encouraged me to say what was on my mind, which was, "Why did you trust this person to be alone with me so much of the time? Didn't his behavior or personality seem at all suspicious to you at any point? Did you honestly not suspect anything weird was going on? If so, why not?" As much as I wished I could ask her these things with equanimity and compassion, the honest truth was that I felt angry, and that anger was obvious when I spoke.

Logically, I knew it was okay and even necessary to feel my feelings, even if they temporarily caused this family member pain. I even knew that we needed to have this discussion if our relationship was going to heal and if I was going to learn to relate to her in a way that allowed me to be completely myself. Still, emotionally, it was extremely difficult for me to do. But the therapist encouraged me to feel the feelings and say the words that needed to be said. He also encouraged my older relative to hear what I was saying so we could move forward into healing.

Unfortunately, my family member was not able to express any emotional response other than defensiveness. She didn't want to hear about my pain. I can't remember her exact words, but in effect she expressed that she felt she had dealt with her feelings about my abuse already, and she wasn't willing to revisit the subject ever again. We left the appointment on an unsettled note. After we left the room, I told her we could continue to have a relationship, but only if she could go to therapy with me until we established a healthier dynamic.

A week or two later, I received a handwritten letter from this family member, and she was angry. She felt that I had embarrassed her in front of the therapist and that I had given her an ultimatum: go to therapy with me or you can't be in my life; my way or the highway. She said she *did* want to have a relationship with me, but not if I ever embarrassed her like that again, and definitely not if I stuck to my guns about my desire to continue with therapy.

In a way, I *did* give her an ultimatum: I set a boundary. I sort of *did* say "my way or the highway." And even though I haven't communicated with this formerly extremely close relative since that time, I'd do the same thing all over again.

It wasn't simple, though. It confused me quite a lot. After an entire life of putting this particular family member's feelings above my own, I couldn't quite believe that I was doing the right thing in setting that boundary. I couldn't completely distance myself from her view of me as a selfish, ungrateful child. So I scheduled another appointment with my childhood counselor. I told him about the letter from my older relative and asked him if he approved of my decision to cut off communication with her. When he expressed his opinion that my choices were valid, I was immensely relieved. Because on my own, I couldn't quite see the forest for the trees. So having a neutral third party with whom I could discuss the situation was immensely valuable.

I'm telling this story to illustrate that setting boundaries isn't always easy or pleasant, and that—because you can't control the reactions of others—the results may not always be picture-perfect according to your expectations or the expectations of the world. But as I mentioned, if I had it to do over, I wouldn't change a thing. Even though it's painful to know that this person who was such a huge part of my life was and is extremely unenthusiastic about honoring my boundary, not communicating with her at all is much less emotionally problematic for me than continuing our unhealthy dynamic. Once I began prioritizing my own emotions over hers, everything else in my life changed in a positive and empowering way. Even though it's an ongoing journey, I began honoring my boundaries and honoring myself more in general. I stared listening to myself, trusting myself, standing my ground, and feeling so much more at home in the world.

That was an extreme boundary-setting story. Here's a more everyday one. During the writing of this chapter, I attended a holiday party where there was a white elephant gift exchange. While I knew the couple throwing the party and five of the other guests very well, the rest of the group was made up of people I had either only met once or had just met that night. When it was my turn to open a gift, one of the items in the gift bag I randomly chose was a bottled alcoholic beverage, and the woman who brought that particular gift declared to the party that by receiving that gift, it meant I had to chug the entire bottle right then and there. I looked around confusedly. I *had* to slam a warm bottle of malt liquor. The gift-giver was adamant that *yes*, I absolutely *had* to. The problem was that I emphatically didn't *want* to. The very thought of taking a single sip of it made me feel gross, and anyway, my drive home was over an hour and I had already had a cocktail. My response was not suave or memorable, and was actually quite awkward, but I did manage to decline. Cringing apologetically, I said something like, "I just really don't feel like it. It doesn't sound good to me right now. But thank you." (Thank you?) Luckily, the moment eventually ended, and the game moved on.

I'm not imagining that particular gift-giver and I are ever going to be buddies. And that's totally fine with me. Perhaps if I had hidden my reluctance and chugged the drink, a friendship could have been in our future (provided I had made it home in one piece). But the only reason I would prefer that scenario would be if I valued her opinion of me over my own happiness, comfort, and well-being. As for the other party guests, despite my inelegance, I'm glad they witnessed me speaking up for myself rather than ignoring my feelings and going along with the "rule." Naturally, after the party, I thought of a number of much smoother ways I could have responded to the situation, such as "I'm going to pass, but you're welcome to it," or even a friendly but resolute "Nope!" Regardless, I'd choose temporary social awkwardness over disrespecting myself and overriding what feels right to me any day. And anyway, if any of my new acquaintances at the party and I are ever going to become better friends, I want them to know who I actually am. I don't want to win their friendship by impressing them with my ability to fit in and go along.

Action Step
• BOUNDARY AUDIT •

While sitting near your self-love altar with your journal or notebook, make a list of your primary relationships. Take a moment with each and ask yourself: do I feel in tune with my own emotions and desires when I'm with this person? Do I feel safe speaking up about what's true for me? Or do I prioritize their emotions and desires over my own? (If you end up feeling drained or uncomfortable after hanging out with them, that's an important clue. For example, before I realized I was in an unhealthy pattern with the female relative in the story above, I used to develop a headache almost every time I spent time with her.)

If you identify one or more relationships in which you regularly lose your sense of yourself, or value the other person so much that you forget to value yourself, lovingly consider ways you might remedy this dynamic. Perhaps you can make a point of breathing consciously and checking in with your body and emotions while you are around this person so you can begin to have a frame of reference for how you actually feel when you are around them. Or, perhaps you might realize that you need to have a heart-to-heart with that person, ask them to go to therapy with you (as I did), or even let that relationship go. If you're not sure, feel into it and let yourself learn as you go. There's no need to take drastic action right away, as long as you do your best to tune into yourself and honor what's true for you, with a sense of curiosity and the comfort of knowing you'll be looking out for yourself to the best of your ability from this time forward.

In general, wherever you are and whomever you're with, do your best to remember that you're safe because you have your own back. If someone suggests that you do something that you really don't want to do, remember that you can brave any temporary awkwardness and decline. If someone subtly or overtly pressures you to do or say something that doesn't feel authentic, see if you can notice this pressure and override it in order to put yourself first. If you get the sense that speaking up for yourself or taking action according to your intuition will not be received positively in certain company, notice this and consider how to move forward in a way that feels authentic to you, whether that involves leaving the relationship(s) or beginning to show your true colors and seeing what happens.

Remember: this is a process. Be patient with yourself and don't feel like you need to do it perfectly. If you realize after the fact that you violated your own boundaries by doing or saying something that wasn't in alignment with your truth, or if you realize you could have handled something in a different way, congratulate yourself for the fact that you noticed. Then, lovingly coach yourself on how you might handle a similar situation in the future.

Seven
ENERGETIC
SELF-CARE

In the last chapter, we explored what it means to set boundaries in the most obvious and straightforward of ways. We talked about tuning into yourself, honoring your needs and desires, and speaking up about what does and doesn't feel right to you.

But boundaries are multidimensional and multilayered, and there is more to them than meets the eye. In this chapter, we'll discuss ways you can take care of yourself by working with your personal energy: the invisible field that fills, surrounds, and radiates out from your body like diamond light shining from a magical lamp. When you become aware of this field, you will begin to sense your ability to take care of it so that it serves as a bubble of energy that can protect you from negativity and awaken to your intuitive guidance system. Just as setting boundaries (as we discussed in the last chapter) will naturally support your energetic well-being, working directly with your energy field will positively affect your ability to set boundaries. It's a holistic boomerang and positive feedback loop.

There are countless additional benefits to becoming aware of, and consciously attending to, your personal energy field, which is also known as your aura. By taking care of your aura, you will support your physical, mental, and emotional health, and you can even consciously expand your openness to positive conditions such as wealth, romance, and success. What's more, regularly attending to your energy field is a profound expression of self-love that assists you in opening up to more and more self-love over the course of your life.

Even if the whole idea of an "aura" or "energy field" seems way out and woo-woo to you right now, if you give the information in this chapter a chance, you'll soon discover these benefits firsthand. Understand: the whole point of taking care of your personal energy field is practical, not religious. In other words, it's not about believing in the objective reality of the energetic realm; rather, it's about using the power of your mind to positively affect your overall wellness: mental, emotional, and physical. (Of course, when you discover how much positive change energy work can set in motion, believing in energy will likely be a natural result. But believing is certainly not necessary or in any way the point.)

Feng Shui

You might say that feng shui is a way of arranging and interacting with your home to create positive change in your life. While you may not think of your décor and home environment when you think of your personal energy field, you should! Once I started learning about and putting feng shui into practice, I felt a more palpable shift in my aura and overall well-being than I ever had before—so much so that I enrolled in feng shui school shortly thereafter and began a private feng shui practice. But there's no need for you to go that far! In this section, you'll find some general guidelines that will help you improve and fine-tune the vibes in your home in a way that you will immediately be able to feel.

Creating a space that nourishes you is a profound act of self-love, and one that supports you day after day and night after night. Wherever you live now—whether it's a trailer, a mansion, an apartment, a basement, a penthouse, or someone else's couch, you can always choose to accept it, love it, and make the very most of it so that you can instantly begin to thrive.

Since you already cleared your clutter in chapter 4, you are ahead of the game when it comes to feng shui. Rule number one in creating a positive vibration in your home is to live with what you love, and, by extension, to *not* live with what you *don't* love. Since we're talking about energy in this chapter, you might like to imagine everything you own as connected to you with a cord of energy: this simply is a way of visualizing your relationship to the item. Then you can imagine that each item is either giving you energy or draining you of energy. Very few items (if any) are neutral in this regard. Either an item makes your life easier, more comfortable, or more beautiful, or it drains you by taking up space, requiring upkeep, or simply dragging you down a little by obstructing the naturally buoyant quality of your home environment.

Something to keep in mind is that—like so much else in this book—clearing clutter is a lifelong habit. Even after I've done the most thorough clutter-clearing imaginable, after as little as a month or two, condiments expire, cupboards and drawers fall into disarray, and I discover clothes in my closet that I no longer want to wear. With this in mind, if you can think of any areas in your home that could use a clutter-clearing tune-up (or if the whole place could use one), take the time you need to clear what needs to be cleared and organize what needs to be organized.

Action Step
• FENG SHUI CHECK-IN •

For this exercise, you will simply be opening your eyes to your home. Ask yourself: is it comfortable? Does it make you smile? Does it inspire you? Are you maximizing its potential to be an expression of self-love? Here are some specific areas to examine when contemplating your answers to these questions:

- Do you move through your home with ease? Could you rearrange or shift anything so that it's easier to move through an average day? (For example, by making things you use regularly more accessible or getting rid of furniture that regularly injures you or makes you uncomfortable?)

- Do all your doors open all the way, without sticking or creaking or hitting something? Life feels easier and hassles seem to magically disappear when you don't store things behind doors in a way that obstructs their full range of motion, and when your doors and locks don't stick. Creaky doors can also represent annoyances and hold them in place, so oil that hinge if you need to.

- Does your artwork make you smile and/or inspire you? And does it all depict something that you would like to experience in your life? Imagery is powerful, and we will subconsciously begin to internalize and play out any dramas or challenges that we even peripherally pick up on in a painting, photo, or sculpture that we see every day in our environment.

- Do you have to crouch to see your entire face and head in any mirror? If so, this may be subtly undermining your self-respect. It's important to easily see your entire head (including the very top of your head) in any mirror on your wall, without having to bend or bow or scrunch in any way.

- Is your bed comfortable? What about your chairs and anywhere you regularly spend time in the home? This is a very clear and obvious opportunity to love yourself, and to regularly receive that love: give yourself the gift of comfort and ease no matter where you are in your home.

- Take a good look at the places you habitually sit or recline in your home: can you see the main door to the room from these places, at least peripherally? When you can, it means you're sitting (or lying) in the power position. If you're not in the power position in any area where you regularly spend time, rearrange the furniture so that you are. If this is not possible, you can approximate the power position by placing a mirror in such a way that you are able to see the main door to the room. (Incidentally, this is also a good idea to do in your workspace. Even if you work in a cubicle, you can position a mirror so that you can see the door to your space behind you.) It sounds like a little detail, but being able to see the door is actually a huge deal when it comes to feeling comfortable, grounded, confident, and at home in your body and life. These feelings naturally carry over into the rest of your life—even when you're not sitting in your home.

- Are all your houseplants healthy? If not, do your best to bring them back to a state of vibrant health. If this proves too challenging, give them to a plant whisperer friend or release them from their constant struggle by giving them back to the earth.

- And if you don't have any houseplants, would you like some? Or if you only have a few, would you like some more? Living with healthy houseplants adds oxygen to the environment, cleans the air, and psychologically reminds you that you live in a safe and hospitable place. (If you have pets, make sure to get houseplants that are not toxic to them. You can do a web search to find lists of plants that are toxic and nontoxic to both cats and dogs.)

- Finally, when you look around your home, does it reflect love back to you? Look for little things you can do in your home to help you feel more pampered and treasured. This will be different for everyone, but to give you some examples, keeping a bowl of fresh fruit on your counter is a little luxury but it can make a big difference in how luxurious you feel. Maybe a plush new bath towel will help you feel more like you're in a day spa than your old bleach-stained one. If your mattress isn't totally comfortable, you could get a new one, or if that's too pricey right now, maybe you could find a high-quality memory foam pad that helps you get a better night's sleep.

The term *feng shui* directly translates to "wind / water." This is possibly because feng shui, like both wind and water, is about flow: in the case of feng shui, it's about how your energy and attention flow when you're in your home. Can you feel your enthusiasm flow upward like a fountain, and swirl gently and buoyantly like a feather in a fresh breeze?

Don't be intimidated by all the feng shui "rules" that you may hear or read about or believe that it's just too complex or extensive for you to grasp. After all, feng shui is ultimately all about *you*: about how you feel in your space and how you can alter it in order to feel even better, and to help yourself feel like the precious and worthy being you are.

You'll find that living in a space you love and that nourishes your spirit with beauty, comfort, and positive energy is a powerful foundation for learning about self-love and putting it into practice. Even if all you can do is shift one or two things right now, when you do so with the intention to treat yourself like a rare and precious orchid, you'll be cultivating a rich and fertile soil in which to grow.

Energetic Hygiene

I'm originally from a small, rural town in the agricultural region of California known as the San Joaquin Valley. It's a town where you could, if you wanted to, walk from one side of town to the other in no more than an hour. It's also a town where my grandparents and the grandparents of many of my peers were buddies in grade school, so a lot of neighbors were sort of like family. It's a quiet place, and a flat one: at any given edge of town, you could see for miles across tomato fields, almond orchards, and grasslands.

When I moved to Los Angeles when I was eighteen, to say it was a culture shock would be an understatement. Even when I later ended up living there for over a decade, there wasn't a day that passed in which I felt completely at ease or at home. I could never get my head around the concept of so many people being in one place, and my nervous system couldn't quite adjust to so much constant movement and noise. What's more, it was extremely difficult to process all the gazes from strangers and all the opinions so many of them felt bold enough to express about my outfit, body, smile, or "vibe."

But as uncomfortable as I so often felt, I wouldn't trade that time of my life for a lot of reasons. One of those reasons is the energetic hygiene practice I was driven—by necessity—to develop and adopt as a regular habit. It was a saving grace that helped me feel as grounded, calm, and comfortable in my own skin as I could manage in such a frenetic place. What exactly *is* "energetic hygiene"? You might say it's a way of clearing and shielding your personal energy field daily, in order to establish a clear awareness of where you end and other people begin. It's also a way of getting in the habit of checking in with how you're feeling—mind, body, and spirit—and using your clear intention in order to improve your feelings as desired. Finally, it's a way of enforcing your boundaries with clear visualizations and intentions.

The best way to understand what energetic hygiene is, however, is to experience it firsthand. Here's a great way to start.

Action Step
• SIMPLE CENTERING AND BALANCING MEDITATION •

Set a timer for five minutes. Sit comfortably on a cushion, couch, or chair with your spine relatively straight in a comfortable way. Close your eyes and take three deep breaths, at any pace that's comfortable for you. Then, let your breath be natural, and simply take note of it. Notice as you breathe in and notice as you breathe out. As you do this, you'll begin to inhabit your body more fully. As a result, you'll notice places where you're holding tension, and you may notice that your breathing is somewhat shallow or tense. There's nothing wrong with any of this. Try not to judge it. Simply notice it. You can even say an inner "yes" to whatever you notice. Your mind will almost certainly begin to wander and to think about any number of things besides your breath. No matter how long your mind has been wandering, this is totally okay too. Whenever you notice it, just bring your awareness right back to your breath: notice when you're breathing in and notice when you're breathing out. If you continue with this for even just a minute or two, you'll begin to naturally relax, and your breath will naturally begin to deepen. You'll also start to feel your energy field. You'll feel a conscious aliveness flowing through your body on the current of the breath, like waves washing in and out over the sand. Continue until the timer lets you know you're finished.

This alone is an amazing way to balance and ground your personal energy field. It brings immediate calm to your mind and even helps heal your body by relaxing it and nourishing it with oxygen and awareness.

It's worth mentioning that as you continue with this practice, you will notice emotions coming up. They may or may not seem to be attached to anything specific. Simply notice these as well and let them move through. These are old emotions that have been previously stuck in your body and energy field, coming up to be washed away and released. It's like rinsing a glass with water, only instead of water, you're using conscious breath to move those old emotions up and out.

Even though this is a beginning practice to help you get in touch with and balance your personal energy field, it's a practice that's worth coming back to daily throughout your life. It's also the perfect way to begin any additional meditation or energetic hygiene practices (like the ones that follow). Over time, you won't

have to set a timer, because you'll feel and sense when you're sufficiently grounded and present (although setting a timer can be
good when you want to employ the practice as a simple meditation and mindfulness practice). It's really up to you. You'll start
to discover what works for you, and your daily practices may
change over time as you modify them to keep yourself interested
and to stay awake to your present-moment needs.

Once you've employed the simple centering meditation for
a day or two, you're ready to add another step: anchoring and
shielding in light. Here's how to do it.

Action Step
• ANCHORING AND SHIELDING IN LIGHT •

Once you've centered and balanced your energy as above, begin
to feel your weight on the earth. Feel the exquisite simplicity
of gravity anchoring you into the chair or the floor. Continue
breathing consciously as you sense your personal energy field as a
blindingly bright, golden-white light. Sense this light within your
every organ and cell, your bones, your skin, and the area around
your body, as well, so that you are seeing and imagining yourself
as a sphere of golden-white light, like the sun.

Now, from your tailbone, imagine you're sending a root or
pillar of light deep down into the earth. Become aware of your
energy field extending deep down in this way until it reaches
the very center of the earth—the earth's core—which you can
imagine as a sort of intensely powerful, intensely bright, subter-
ranean sun. Allow your root or pillar of light to enter into this
ball of energy at the earth's core. As it does, the earth's anchoring, empowering light moves up your pillar naturally, like a rapid
upwelling of liquid light. Be aware that this is natural: this is how

this energy naturally wants to flow, just like a spring of water flows up to the surface of the earth from deep down below. See and sense the earth's energy moving up, up, up, into your tailbone, feet, and legs, and then up through your belly, solar plexus, back, chest, arms, hands, shoulders, neck, face, brain, and scalp.

Next, from the crown of your head, imagine you are sending a trunk or a pillar of light straight up into the sky. Sense this pillar or trunk moving up, up, up, out of the earth's atmosphere, where you can envision it entering the diamond-white light of Infinity. Sense this energy turn into a funnel, where it connects with this infinite, living light. In your mind's eye, see this light naturally and rapidly flowing downwards, and entering the crown of your head, where it merges and mixes with the golden-white light of your personal energy field and the light of the earth. It moves through your scalp, brain, face, throat, shoulders, heart, arms, hands, solar plexus, back, belly, tailbone, legs, and feet.

Now you can mentally check in with the sphere of light that is your personal energy field, and sense how it is anchored in both the earth and the cosmos.

At this point, it's a good idea to call on the Divine, or the Infinite Intelligence, in a way that feels powerful for you. I like to call on Archangel Michael, but this does not need to be in any way denominational or religious. You can call on Universal Love, Infinity, or any name you prefer for the pure power that (to paraphrase author and scholar Joseph Campbell) transcends all levels of rational thought. Ask this Intelligence to clear and vacuum your energy field of any stuck or challenging energies, including any grudges, grievances, old pain, guilt, blocks, stuck emotions, or limiting beliefs. You can imagine this Infinite Intelligence sending in a vacuum tube of light that powerfully removes anything that is standing in the way of your energetic wellness. (It's not necessary to take an inventory of, or even to have an inkling of, exactly what's being vacuumed away. Simply request the removal of anything that doesn't serve you.) Relax and allow this clearing.

Once this feels complete (it shouldn't take very long), ask Infinite Intelligence to completely fill and surround you with shielding light, in which only love remains, through which only love may enter. Sense this light further balancing and healing you and filling in and repairing any areas in your energy field that may need extra support. Imagine a sphere of even brighter light than before completely filling and surrounding you and gently spinning in a clockwise direction to keep the protection strong. (When you're working with energy, it can be helpful to remember the phrase, "Lefty loosey, righty tighty." In other words, when energy spins clockwise, it locks something in or increases a particular type of energy. When energy spins counterclockwise, it unwinds, loosens, and disperses energy.)

It's important to note that this bubble of light is not like a wall, shutting you off from connection with others. Rather, it's a way of staying grounded and protected in positive energy, and in the energy you choose. It's a way of sensing your personal space, so that when you encounter other people and energies as you go about your day, you can feel perfectly safe, and you can more easily perceive what does and doesn't feel like it aligns with who you are and how you want to feel and be in the world.

Throughout the day, you can quickly refresh this bubble of light no matter where you are or what you are doing. To do so, simply call once more on the Divine or Infinite Intelligence in your preferred manner and request another quick clearing with the vacuum tube of light. Follow up by requesting a refill of golden-white light, within and around you. Visualize the sphere cocooning you and spinning gently in a clockwise direction.

If you feel ungrounded, spacey, or frazzled throughout the day, you can always take a moment to ground and center your energy by noticing your breathing, acknowledging the downward pull of gravity, and remembering the anchoring pillar or roots of light that connect your energy field to the core of the earth.

And if you want to refresh your perspective or intuition, or to bring in a constant and sustained flow of enthusiasm and inspiration, you can remember the pillar or trunk of light that connects your energy field to the infinite light of the cosmos.

Everyday Action Steps
• TAKE CARE OF YOUR ENERGY •

Before we move on from the topic of energetic self-care, I want to mention a few other things it will benefit you to keep in mind.

When you spend time with someone, notice and honor how your body, mind, and spirit feel during and after your time together. For example, if you notice that you often seem to have a headache or stomach cramps while you're with a particular family member or friend, or if you often feel drained or unsettled after you leave them, it's likely this is not a coincidence. With curiosity and compassion, take a moment when you're alone to take some deep breaths and tune in deeply to the energetic dynamic behind this symptom or symptoms. It's possible you've been pushing down your True Self in some way by ignoring your intuition or putting someone else's opinions above yours. Use your conscious breathing and energetic hygiene techniques to deeply tap into what will most benefit you as you move forward in this relationship. Most likely it will involve some combination of setting a boundary, speaking your truth, or even (in some cases) letting go of the relationship altogether.

Remember that none of this is about you passing judgment on someone. Rather, it's about you taking care of yourself and listening to the inner resonance of what is true for you. You don't have to say, "Oh, that person is a psychic vampire," or, "That person has bad vibes." It's not about the other person being good or bad, and it's not about you being crabby or nice. It's about you being honest with yourself about what does and does not nourish your soul. It's your life! Spend it being honest with yourself and others and spending time with people who celebrate you for being you.

If you have access to a bathtub, every now and then, it can be a helpful energetic self-care practice to dissolve two cups of Epsom salt and a tablespoon or two of sea salt in a warm bath and soak. (Make sure to have plenty of drinking water on hand so you can stay hydrated.) This will neutralize and disperse negative energy and help you feel grounded, centered, relaxed, and recharged. It's especially helpful for times when you feel drained or imbalanced, or any time you want to boost your personal radiance and energetic well-being. Bonus: it also helps you sleep.

Speaking of sleep, **getting a good night's sleep regularly boosts every aspect of your well-being: physical, mental, emotional, and spiritual.** If this has been an issue for you in the past, do your best to turn your sleep challenges around. This may involve cutting back on caffeine or only drinking it early in the morning, clearing clutter out of your bedroom, making your bed more comfortable, making sure your bedroom is extra dark, turning off your phone before bed, and making sure you've had enough to eat. Another important and often overlooked consideration when it comes to getting enough sleep is what's called sleep hygiene. Sleep hygiene means getting to bed at the same time and waking up at the same time regularly so that you give yourself eight full hours of "sleep opportunity" every night. It sounds simple, but many sleep experts say that over time it's one of the best tools for training your body to get its full allotment of sleep. It's also worth mentioning that, according to author and sleep expert Dr. Matthew Walker in *Why We Sleep*, 65°F is the optimal temperature for deep sleep, and keeping your feet warm is also conducive to rest.[8]

While the term *self-care* has become so much of a buzzword in recent years that its potency has become somewhat diluted, when you precede the term with "energetic," you'll find it becomes easier to sense both its meaning and its importance. In other words, once you develop an awareness of your personal energy field, and then you prioritize your energetic well-being, you'll intuitively know what will heal, nourish, and benefit you, as well as what won't. As you move through the remainder of this book (and your life!), let your relationship with your personal energy deepen. Listen to it, be curious about it, and honor it. Allow it to inform your lifelong commitment to treating yourself like the precious being you are.

---

8. Matthew Walker, *Why We Sleep: Unlocking the Power of Sleep and Dreams*, (New York: Simon and Schuster, 2017).

Eight
EXCEPTIONALLY ORDINARY

In the Harry Potter movie *The Half-Blood Prince* there's a scene where Luna Lovegood repairs Harry's broken nose. He then asks her how he looks, and she answers definitively, "Exceptionally ordinary,"[9] which is a beautiful turn of phrase.

For so many years, I thought I had to be exceptionally *extra*ordinary: i.e., refreshingly out of the box, devastatingly beautiful, and breathtakingly brilliant. (Not to mention an excellent dancer, hilarious storyteller, fascinating party guest, knower of surprisingly obscure trivia, and the most loyal of all friends.) Even while I was terrified of not being at the highest point of every curve, in my honest heart of hearts, I probably suspected I was more likely to fall into the ordinary range in all

---

9. *Harry Potter and the Half-Blood Prince,* directed by David Yates (Warner Bros, 2009).

those areas, which was likely true. But I couldn't admit that to myself, out of terror of disappearing into the background of life forever, being woefully unloved, and finally blowing away into obscurity like ashes in the wind. Life was a constant struggle against the truth of my ordinariness. It was exhausting.

If I were telling you this over coffee, as a friend, you might say, "But Tess: you *are* extraordinary! Here are all the ways I see you that way [insert compliments here]." And those would be very nice things for you to say as a friend. You would probably even mean them! And some of them might be true in a way. But they wouldn't be absolutely true, or true in any meaningful sense. Or, let's put it this way: even if they were true, it wouldn't matter. I would rather just assume that I'm ordinary, right across the board, and that you are too. And I would want us to embrace that about ourselves.

For the sake of argument, let's say you're an Olympic swimmer, or a Harvard valedictorian, or an Academy Award winner, or the Most Interesting Man in the World. Even then, you are just one more human in a world of billions of humans. As I said a different way in a previous chapter, while some things about you are relatively exceptional, other things about you are below average and others are just plain ordinary. Usually, there's no way to know which is which for absolute certain, just as it's difficult to instantly divine or guess what is exceptional and what is ordinary about any given stranger you pass on the street.

My point is that constantly mining our perception of ourselves for a glittering jewel of ego-satisfaction is a waste of time and an ultimately hollow pursuit. Instead, let's just be ordinary. We can still excel at things! And we can still have remarkable experiences. But by embracing our ordinariness, we will free up our mind energy to focus on actually enjoying being who we are instead of constantly seeking to bask in our extraordinariness.

When you embrace being ordinary, you can fully revel in the present moment, exactly as it is. Celebrating your (exceptional) ordinariness allows you to be present with what you are doing, and the wonderful beings in front of you, instead of wishing you were doing yoga on a yacht with a Silicon Valley tech wizard or drinking sangria on a private jet with Middle Eastern royalty. (Incidentally, as glittery as they may seem at first, eventually even those people and activities would also, eventually, reveal themselves to be ordinary.)

The Invisible Kingdom

Some years ago, I stumbled upon an obscure fairy tale called "The Invisible Kingdom."[10] It's about a guy named George who lived in a little house outside a village. He was nicknamed "dreamy George" because after he finished working in the fields, he loved to sit on an ancient millstone for hours and gaze out at the beautiful valley, the river that ran through it, and the mountains on the far side of the river. When he did this, nature came alive and began to sing to him.

One day as he sat on the millstone, thinking about how no one in his village understood him, feeling isolated and lonely, he fell asleep and dreamt a beautiful princess appeared on a golden swing, showering roses upon him. When he awoke, the roses were all around him. Besotted and understandably convinced that she was real, he went out in search of the princess.

---

10. Richard Leander, "The Invisible Kingdom," *Wonder-World: A Collection of Fairy Tales, Old and New* (London: George Bell and Sons, 1875).

After a number of days, he came upon a forest where the clouds hung especially close to the earth. There, he discovered two guys assaulting a bearded old man, whom George wasted no time in rescuing. The old man turned out to be the King of Dreams, and the guys attacking him were minions of the King of Reality. The King of Dreams, relieved, opened a trap door in the ground and led George deep into a beautiful underground world with floating castles and clouds.

While the King of Dreams showed George around, George was overjoyed to run into the princess who had visited him in his dream. He and the princess rushed into each other's arms and temporarily forgot about the King because they were so happy to see each other. Then, George looked at the King and demanded he stay with the princess. He basically said either he was staying or she was coming with him, and that was how it had to be.

Feeling indebted, the King of Dreams allowed George to take the dream princess back up through the trap door and into the world of reality above. When George expressed concern that the princess would be without a kingdom, the King agreed to give George a kingdom, but explained that he didn't have any visible ones to offer: only invisible ones. George couldn't imagine what an invisible kingdom might be but took what he could get.

After exiting the trapdoor with the princess, George found himself instantly on the old millstone on his property, with the princess beside him. As they held hands and gazed together at the beauty of the river and mountains, a thin map dropped out of the sky that showed them the lay of the land of their very own kingdom. "And when they looked at their little cottage, behold it had become a wonderful castle, with glass steps, and marble walls, and the carpets were made of velvet... when they entered, the servants bowed respectfully; trumpets sounded, and page boys went in front of them and strewed flowers in the way."[11]

The next day, the whole village heard that George was back and had brought a wife with him. They gossiped among themselves about how plain she was and how ragged her clothing. They couldn't see that she was a beautiful princess any more than they could see that George's house had become a palace. George "did not bother himself [about the opinions of the townsfolk] but lived with his princess very happily in his kingdom. And they had six children, each one more beautiful than the last, and they were all princes and princesses."[12]

"The Invisible Kingdom" is my favorite fairytale. I love it because it perfectly describes the alchemical magic of embracing an "ordinary" life. Or rather, of embracing your actual experience of your life, rather than how other people perceive it. While George's house is not fancy, his connection with nature and his dreamy perspective allow him to see the magic in the everyday. When he finds a wife who sees that with him, their outwardly mundane life taps into an inner vein of gold. It's not a kind of gold that glitters in the eyes of the townsfolk or indeed anyone other than George and his family. But George doesn't mind a bit, because to him, he is king of his world, and he sees his family as the precious and beautiful beings they actually are.

In Los Angeles, where I lived for almost twenty years, I observed an endless striving for extraordinariness. In many circles, it seemed to be the cultural norm to find ways to differentiate yourself and rise above the mediocre masses: perhaps by

---

11. Richard Leander, "The Invisible Kingdom," *Wonder-World: A Collection of Fairy Tales, Old and New* (London: George Bell and Sons, 1875), 167.

12. Leander, "The Invisible Kingdom," 167.

being the thinnest, or by wearing ridiculously expensive jeans, or by getting to skip the line at the new "it" club.

It didn't take me long to discover the profound desperation embedded in this value system. I got the sense that the people who were most invested in it were the very opposite of how they would like to appear. Beneath their veneer of being fabulous, confident, and on top of the world, many of them seemed to feel wounded, lonely, hollow, and unworthy of true happiness or satisfaction.

When I was twenty-one, I attended a party at the Playboy Mansion with a rich, much older man I barely knew. After inhaling cocaine and promptly throwing up in the bathroom, I stepped out, looked around, and realized that nothing was happening that I wanted to be a part of. I saw glittery people laughing and posing but had no desire to participate. So many people thought this was the place to be, but as I stood there, I felt nothing. Or to be more specific, it was as if I was drowning in an endless abyss of deep, dark nothing. Afterward, I instructed my date's limo driver to take me straight home to my tiny apartment in a poorer area of town, which I suddenly craved like a glass of water in the desert. As the limo pulled away from my dark and litter-strewn curb, impossibly close to the freeway, I gazed up at the cracked cement steps to my apartment, indescribably happy to be home.

As a small-town girl, I had imagined finding myself at an exclusive party at the Playboy Mansion would be some sort of apotheosis: a teleportation to Olympus, a graduation to the rarified realm of the gods. At the time, the Playboy Mansion was (to fellow middle-class members of my generation) considered to be the height of luxurious exclusivity, and I thought being a party guest there would mean I had finally escaped the monotony, "made it," and elevated myself above the mediocre masses. In fact, none of that carried the last bit of truth. The whole experience was the complete opposite of

Dreamy George's invisible kingdom, which brought him immense joy as he saw his everyday world as the most precious of realms. Dreamy George's kingdom was not in any way meant to impress the outside world or to measure up to some external standard, but rather to infuse his actual life experience with meaning, beauty, connection, and love. Looking back on life from your deathbed, which would you rather have: impressive bragging rights about flashy parties you went to, or real, nourishing relationships and moment-to-moment joy?

Perhaps you've had a similar experience in which you realized that the "it" party or job or status symbol was nothing more than a sparkly mirage. If you haven't, though, it may be that you are thinking, in some part of your mind, that my experience at the Playboy Mansion *was* actually glamorous and desirable and that I am being either deluded or falsely modest to describe it as something I didn't like. How do I know this? Because this is what *I* would have thought before I had the experience myself. The cultural conditioning I was swimming in wouldn't have allowed me to think anything else.

To be perfectly honest, that one experience did not completely cure me of my starry-eyed striving for social status. But it did chip away at it. It did open the door.

At any rate, if I haven't effectively convinced you that an everyday life of joy is better than a photogenic party filled with celebrities and cocaine, that's okay. Believe me: I get it. But don't let that stop you from reading on. I still think I can persuade you.

Adopt, Don't Shop

Have you ever adopted an adult animal from a pound, shelter, or rescue organization? I have. My late cat, Acorn, and I met many years ago when she was in a cage at a rescue event in a park in Glendale, California. Her skinny, fluffy little body was quaking as she looked at me fearfully with her giant eyes. She was one of the "last chance" animals from the pound: if she hadn't been adopted at this event, she would have been euthanized. As you may or may not know, puppies and kittens are pretty easy for organizations to find homes for. It's the fully-grown animals that are much more difficult to place.

Acorn had a whole life before she met me, with, I was told, at least one prior home who had rejected her or given her up for whatever reason. When I brought her home, she had a scary-sounding cough, and she was so sick she refused to eat. The vet instructed me to give her antibiotics regularly, which I did, until she—luckily—regained her appetite and health.

While kittens and puppies are obviously precious and wonderful, there's something profoundly heart-opening about giving a grown animal a second chance at a happy life. Once Acorn was bright-eyed and spry, she was the most loving and loyal friend I've ever known. She had a sweet and gentle energy that everyone who met her commented on. She would almost never miss a chance to curl up on my lap and purr. And knowing that her past had been filled with abandonment and a brush with euthanasia bonded me to her all the more.

Your relationship with yourself can be just the same. Instead of buying into the subtle yet relentless societal messages that tell you that you are a product that must be endlessly improved upon if you ever hope to be loved and desirable, adopt yourself exactly as you are, *right now*. If you're (metaphorically) shaking in a cage, with kennel cough, with a past history of rejection and neglect, all the more reason to gather yourself up in a blanket and nurse yourself back to health. Just like Acorn, you couldn't be any more deserving of love if you tried.

Persian cats, labradoodles, French bulldogs, and other animals who have been bred have of course done nothing wrong and are just as worthy of our love as other animals. It wasn't their fault that someone exploited their parents in order to sell them and their siblings for profit. While it may not be the best idea to support puppy mills, kitten mills, or private breeders by purchasing expensive animals, I'm not implying that purebred animals are inherently wrong or the least bit unlovable. I don't want this metaphor to be misconstrued.

Similarly, there is nothing wrong with those among us who have "won the genetic lottery" in that they happened to be born with looks or qualities that bestow privilege upon them in our society. It's not their fault that so many media messages subtly or overtly declare their superiority over the rest of us or paint them as ideals to which we all must aspire. You might even fall into this category in one way or several ways—many of us do. If so, please know that I am not disparaging you for this in the least.

What I *am* getting at is simply that whoever you are, whatever you look like, and whatever your current life situation happens to be, adopt yourself wholeheartedly, just as I adopted Acorn, and just as you may have adopted a beloved furry family member of your own. Don't buy into the media hypnotism that you must shop for "extraordinary" qualities that you don't have but should have. Don't look at someone's defined abs on Instagram and say to yourself, "My abs look nothing like that. Until my abs do look like that, I will not fully accept myself or believe that I deserve love." Don't look at your own Photoshopped face and say, "I won't be happy until my nose is really that pointy or my eyes are actually that wide-set." That is like shopping (rather than adopting) in that it involves buying into the media messages and lusting after qualities you hope will (in the future, perhaps) prove your worthiness rather than opening your heart fully to your present-moment preciousness.

The Little Way

I'm not Catholic, but I love Saint Thérèse of Lisieux. She wrote, "The splendor of the rose and the whiteness of the lily do not take away the perfume of the little violet or the delightful simplicity of the daisy...If all flowers wanted to be roses, nature would lose her springtime beauty..."[13]

Saint Thérèse was actually a great inspiration for a saint who came along a little later: the woman we know as Mother Teresa. Mother Teresa is often credited with the statement, "We cannot all do great things. But we can do small things with great love."[14] This is an echo of Saint Thérèse's "little way," which she wrote about in her book *Story of a Soul*. The "little way" is about letting go of the ego's need to be great in order to do everyday things with a spirit of love and service.

I would say the little way is also about loving the modest apartment where you *do* live rather than the flashy mansion where you don't. It's about caring for your tortoiseshell rescue cat wholeheartedly, without ever for a moment imagining you would love her more if only she were a snowy white Persian kitten. It's about putting your whole heart into the job you have today even if you're also taking steps toward getting (or creating) the job you want tomorrow. If you're a rose, it's about being that. And if

---

13. St. Thérèse of Lisieux, *Story of a Soul: the Autobiography of St. Thérèse of Lisieux* (Washington, DC: ICS Publications, 2013), 14.

14. Michelle Van Loon, *Becoming Sage: Cultivating Meaning, Purpose, and Spirituality in Midlife* (Chicago: Moody Press, 2020), 165.

you're a daisy or a violet or a dandelion, it's about being that too. Embrace the little way and share your unique beauty and perfume with the world. We don't want a homogenous springtime composed of only roses. We want *all* the flowers to bloom.

Your action step for embracing extraordinary ordinariness is a cinematic one. Before moving onto the next chapter, watch one, two, or (better yet) all three of the following movies.

Action Step
• WATCH A MOVIE •

Fyre: The Greatest Party That Never Happened: If you're one of the millions of people who look at Instagram and imagine that you and/or your social life are somehow deficient because you're not a supermodel drinking a rum cocktail on a tropical island (or whatever), this movie will help disabuse you of this life-stealing notion. As you watch, ask yourself: *Who would I rather be: one of these rain-soaked guests, objectified models, or flashy con artists? Or Dreamy George and his dream princess?*

Will Success Spoil Rock Hunter? 1957 is perhaps not the best year for movies, but *Will Success Spoil Rock Hunter?*, starring the hypnotic Jayne Mansfield, is definitely a gem. It's also incredibly instructive when it comes to recognizing the difference between achieving success in the eyes of the world and assessing success by your own personal measure of authentic joy. I will warn you, however, that the sexism portrayed in this movie runs deep. If you're easily offended by such things, try to remember that the movie was a product of its time, and think of watching it as an honest investigation into the very real history of chauvinism. (If sexism is really triggering for you, you can skip it, but do be aware that it is the quintessential Jayne Mansfield movie, and she was one fascinating woman—so maybe make a note to come back to it one day.)

Less Than Zero: This iconic 1980s movie starring Robert Downey, Jr. goes into some pretty dark places, so if that's not your thing, you'll probably want to skip this one. The reason I recommend it here, though, is because it clearly illustrates the discrepancy that can exist between the *appearance* of flashy wealth and exclusive parties and the actual experience of them. As you watch it, remember Dreamy George. Would he trade his invisible kingdom for the mansions and modeling and expensive drugs portrayed in this film? Nope! Never. Never ever *ever*.

Nine
LET YOUR BODY BE

While the words "I could eat" might not sound particularly profound, they once were to me. It was the day I heard my cousin say them nonchalantly in response to a question like, "Hey, is anyone hungry yet?" The very fact that this three-syllable statement, "I could eat," seemed like no big deal to her is what made it echo in my mind like a song from 2001. I remember feeling so many feelings, like admiration, jealousy, and awe. I wondered: how do you not feel riddled with anxiety at the very mention of food? I tried so hard to imagine what it would feel like.

Even though, when I look back at this moment, I can see how freaked out I was around food and body image, I couldn't have articulated it. At the time, I would have told anyone who asked that I was pretty darn okay with it all. But now that I'm actually okay, I can see how *not* okay I was.

That wasn't that long ago. In fact, at the time of this writing, I've only been finding my way out of what we might call the cult of "wellness" or the dogma of diet culture for less than a year. Maybe you're already out of it, or maybe you were never in it, but if you're like most people, you have no idea what I'm even talking about. Let me explain.

Scientifically, unequivocally, data shows that *diets don't work*. And by "diets," I don't just mean Weight Watchers and Dr. Atkins and Slimfast and Jenny Craig. I mean anything we do to restrict food in any way—including calories, food groups, macronutrients, or specific foods or ingredients—does not actually, in the long term, help us to be thinner *or* healthier. (And thin and healthy are *not* synonymous! More on this in just a moment.) So this includes not just what we call "diets," but what have also come to be called "lifestyles," or "clean eating habits." It definitely includes any form of fasting or "detoxing."

Not only do externally imposed diets (and "lifestyles") not work for weight loss and health in any long-term or sustainable way, they are actually detrimental. I know, I know. If you've never heard this before, it sounds absolutely crazy and very, very wrong. And it may even sound like something you wouldn't want to be true, because it would mean that you've wasted a ton of time and energy and money on a belief that is, essentially, false and even harmful.

But it really is true. Pretty much everyone who attempts to shrink their body by limiting or changing their food intake ends up gaining back anything they may have lost, and often (studies indicate that *over half the time*) they gain back even *more*. Of the people who *do* manage to stay shrunken (a very tiny percentage—less than 5 percent by some estimates), evidence suggests that these people are constantly hungry and obsessing about food to the point where their quality of life is significantly diminished. Is that actually success? Having experienced it myself, I feel pretty confident in answering *no*. All of this adds up to prove the assertion that diets really and truly *never* work. Ever.

You may very well be asking, "But what about health? Isn't it healthier to be slim?" Actually, believe it or not, no. If you look past the hype and the dogma, the actual science says *nope*. While there are certain health challenges that correlate with having a larger body size, there are also some very convincing indicators that freaking out about food and weight is actually more detrimental to our health than having a larger body size. It also seems highly possible that the stress and medical bias caused by weight stigma and fat-phobia could be among the most health-eroding factors of all.

The fact is that genetically, we all have a predetermined healthy weight range. And if we let our bodies tell us what they need rather than mistrusting their cravings and hunger cues, we will, eventually, naturally fall into that weight range.

What's more, diet culture (a pithy name for this particular brand of mass hypnotism) is almost certainly the culprit when it comes to binging and "emotional eating." By teaching us to ignore or mistrust our bodies' cues, our bodies naturally try to rescue us by what they perceive as the threat of starvation by flipping a switch that tells us to eat, eat, eat. Your body can't tell the difference between dieting and an actual famine. Your body also can't tell the difference between the neurological effect of planning to diet and planning for an actual lack of available food. If you think about it, binging is actually a healthy and logical psychological response to the potential for a future with too few calories.

Believe me, when I first heard about all this (which is variously called intuitive eating, the Health at Every Size movement, and the antidiet movement), I was painfully reluctant to believe it, for many reasons. First and foremost, it was such a paradigm shift that I couldn't get my head around it at first. I had been on some sort of restricted diet for literally as long as I could remember. As a child, I was almost never allowed to have candy, soda, or chocolate. When I became a competitive gymnast in elementary school, I began restricting sweets on my own. When I was in high school, our culture's famously ridiculous "fat-free" phase was in full swing, so I restricted anything with more than one or two grams of fat. In my twenties, I tried the Atkins diet and later became a vegan, and even occasionally (when I thought I was being especially "good") a raw vegan. When I was in my late thirties and naturally started putting on a little more weight, I began restricting sugar and calories as well and weighing myself first thing every single morning. Even though I was never out of what the mainstream medical establishment considers a "healthy" weight range for my height, it was during this time that my hair became thinner and duller, my period became irregular, and I had trouble sleeping throughout the night.

Sadly, my story is not unique. So many of us have been restricting for so long, we can't even conceive of another way. Or, if you haven't been restricting, you might think you should be, imagining that you're somehow less virtuous or worthy or deserving of love than people who are. This belief, too, would obviously have a negative psychological effect on your mental and physical health, including your relationship with food and your body.

At the time of this writing, a brand-new year has just begun. Looking back at the intentions I wrote last year, I saw that I had written, "I love my body unconditionally." (I always write my intentions in the present tense.) I don't remember writing that intention, but I'm pretty sure that when I wrote it I was not getting my hopes up that it would actually come true. Even though I held the value of unconditional body positivity, after so many years of restricting foods and withholding love from my body for various appearance-related reasons, I certainly wasn't going to hold my breath.

Looking back over the events of the past year, it intrigues me to see how the Universe went ahead and helped me manifest that intention, despite my cynicism and despite my resistance. In fact, it pretty much dragged me kicking and screaming. First, my podcast cohost told me that she'd been getting into intuitive eating. I didn't say anything then but I thought to myself how terrible it would be if I let myself eat what I intuitively wanted to eat. My weight and "health" obsessions made me shudder at the thought. The very next week, I was reading a book about sexuality (*Come As You Are*—great book!) and the author, Emily Nagoski, PhD, mentioned the Health At Every Size movement and revealed the science that shows that being thin is definitely not all it's cracked up to be as far as health goes and that being underweight is actually more detrimental to your health than being what the mainstream medical establishment would call "overweight." I had never heard this information before.

Also, it seemed like I shouldn't ignore the coincidence that after promptly rejecting the idea of intuitive eating, I would happen to read about it a week later. So I thought, "Maybe I should check this out after all." I told my podcast cohost about my realization and she sent me a link to a podcast she'd been listening to about it (*Food Psych*, hosted by Christy Harrison). I started listening to the episode she sent, and I instantly decided that I hated everything about it.[15] I texted her that it wasn't for me, and she (luckily) gave me one more suggestion, to read *The F*ck It Diet: Eating Should Be Easy* by Caroline Dooner. I wasn't sure if I was going to follow this advice, but when I checked the book out on Amazon, I saw that a reviewer said that when she started reading the book, she began to cry, and as she read the rest of the book, she didn't stop crying. When I saw that review, something told me this was an important book and I wanted to know what it said. I downloaded it to my Kindle and began reading. And finally—mercifully!—it clicked. From that point forward, it has been like a process of being deprogrammed from an insidious cult, of which I have been a lifelong member.

So, hey, if you're like me and you can't get your head around this yet, I get it! If you're shaking your head no and dreading the thought of eating whatever you want whenever you want to, go ahead and ignore this perspective. Write it off. Chalk it up to a woo-woo fad. If it's time for you to learn it and believe it and shift your behavior according to it, though, *it will find you*. So don't be surprised if you hear about it again tomorrow or next week or a month from now. Don't be shocked if it knocks on your door like a Mormon missionary and won't take no for an answer. Because that's what it did for me. And despite my earlier reluctance, I am so grateful it did. Every day.

If you've been restricting (like I was) and you suddenly decide to let your body tell you what it wants and when, at first your eating habits really do look like you fear they will. It's likely you'll eat lots of whatever you had previously been restricting, possibly at all hours of the day and night. And you're also likely eat very little

---

15. Just so you know, now I love the *Food Psych* podcast. I just needed a little more orientation first.

of whatever you held up as the paragon of healthfulness before: raw vegetables, raisins, low-carb protein bars (blech! I ate about a thousand too many of those), date and nut bars, unsweetened yogurt, or whatever. Diet culture would have us believe that this would continue forever until we were beyond saving, drowning in the abyss of our own unhealthiness. But this is not the case! I was astounded to discover that eventually, my body began to crave what it needed and not what it didn't. At first, when I stopped restricting, I ate a ton of chocolate and onion rings and brownies and chips. Mainly. For like a month. Now, I still eat those things, but in moderation. (Not because I consciously moderate but because my body doesn't ask for a huge amount.) I also sometimes crave a whole plate of raw veggies, a bowl of fresh watermelon, a whole grain bagel with nut butter, or any other number of delicious foods. Sometimes I just want a bell pepper.

The point is, now my body is calling the shots rather than my intellectual concepts of nutrition that I read about in some magazine. (Which, if you are alive for a while, you realize change regularly anyway. In the 1990s it was all about fat-free cookies and weird butter-flavored sprinkles. Currently, keto and veganism are both all the rage, and they are in many ways opposites of each other. How is that even logical?) After all these years of distrusting my body's hunger and craving cues, I am continually astounded that my body actually knows what will energize it and nourish it best. It's true! Our bodies actually know! I mean, if you think about it, why wouldn't they? Of *course* they do.

The difference intuitive eating has made in my life is incredible. Profound. Way beyond what I even thought possible. I am happier, more grounded, more energized, more focused, and more at peace with myself. I sleep better, I am more present in my relationships, I am more inspired in my career, and my hair and nails are stronger than they have ever been. Yes, I had to face my fear of weighing more. But once I did, it was so, so, so worth it.

Admittedly, I didn't end up weighing that much more. But even if I did, it would still be worth it. I mean, I got rid of my scale as soon as I realized how unnecessary and even harmful it was, so I don't know an exact number, but I can tell my body is different: more natural and nourished than it was before. And I wouldn't want it any other way. I had previously lived in terror of my naturally round belly and had done everything in my power to flatten it and whittle it down. Now, I sometimes find myself looking at my belly in the mirror and thinking, "This is my body! This is how my body naturally looks." But don't feel pressure to love the way your body looks right away, and don't worry if you don't love it every single day. (I don't! Even though I generally approve of my body, I still have challenging body-image days.) As my friend and intuitive eating coach, Molly Kate Seifert, reminds us, "Loving your body doesn't actually have anything to do with liking how your body physically looks, but rather being fully connected with it, like any loving relationship. While it's a fun perk to start loving and accepting the external appearance, too, that can take some serious time!"

One other surprising benefit I want to mention: my digestion. Before my intuitive eating journey, I had assumed I just had an extra sensitive digestive system. I thought the answer was some combination of eating fewer calories and restricting more types of food. Now, I realize the problem was that I wasn't listening to my body's natural cravings and hunger cues, because now my digestion is better than it's ever been! Did you know that the vast majority of people with disordered eating have digestive issues?

(Perhaps even 98 percent?) Before learning about the antidiet movement, I did not. I had no idea. But yep, it's a fact![16]

I'm still healing and learning to find peace with this new perspective. It's still unsettling to me that I was under such a disempowering illusion for such a big portion of my life. And, now that I'm on the other side of it, it's disconcerting to see how many people are still in it. Any given selection of mainstream magazine covers visible from the supermarket checkout line contain countless headlines about weight loss. It is the norm to shame and attempt to change all body types except one. I am sensitive now to how pervasive fat phobia and thin privilege are in our society, and it's painful to see, especially because I'm so recently out of all this myself. Nobody said changing paradigms was easy.

I don't know about you, but my social media accounts contributed in no small way to my escalating appearance-anxiety and disordered eating. Putting my image up there for everyone to see on a regular basis incited Insta-anxiety and YouTube-terror. I know I'm not alone in this. I recently read an article in *Psychology Today* about how large numbers of very young women are visiting plastic surgeons and asking them to make them look like their own Photoshopped faces. It also seems like no coincidence that the diet and weight loss industries are currently making more money than ever before. (According to some estimates, the diet industry is a sixty- to seventy-billion-dollar enterprise. As body image coach Molly Kate says, "Can you imagine if body love and intuitive eating had that big of a marketing budget? If it did, we could legit change the world!")

---

16. C. Boyd, et al., "Psychological Features Are Important Predictors of Functional Gastrointestinal Disorders in Patients with Eating Disorders," *Scandinavian Journal of Gastroenterology* 40, no. 8 (2005): 929–35.

Action Step
• LOOK BEYOND THE PHOTO •

Bring to mind someone you love. Now pull up a picture of them on your phone. Is that them? No. Who they are and what you love in them is not that stale, electronic likeness of their face. Your love for them has nothing to do with how dewy their skin looks or how much their eyes "pop." It is so, so, so beyond that: so much more important and precious than that. In the exact same way, you are not your picture. And I am not my picture. Pictures are not who we are. We are human beings. We are spirits. We are souls. We are flames, dancing. We are waterfalls, shining in sunlight. We are a flock of birds soaring through a lucent blue sky. We are vibrant green seedlings, sprouting in springtime soil.

To reiterate, here is what we are *not:* electronic images begging desperately for that impersonator of actual human connection known as "likes." So let's divest ourselves of this soul-stealing concept once and for all. Let's be honest: we are the only ones who *can* divest ourselves of this concept. Goddess knows Instagram isn't going to do it for us.

If this is the first time you've heard of the antidiet or Health at Every Size movement, it's probable that this measly little chapter isn't going to cut it and you still have a lot more learning and deprogramming to do. If you feel guided, you may want to read *The F*ck It Diet* by Caroline Dooner and/or *Anti-Diet* by Christy Harrison. Because of the degree of cultural hypnotism, it's hard for me to imagine a person who wouldn't benefit from reading both of these books. Even if you already eat intuitively, learning about just how duped we've all been for so long will likely be illuminating and freeing. Furthermore, depending on your relationship with food and your body, you may also want to get treatment

or find therapy to help you heal. If you suspect you will benefit from having professional support in this area, you can find a
list of therapists, nutritionists, and doctors who get it on Christy
Harrison's website.

Action Step
• BODY LOVE RITUAL •

Regardless of your current relationship with food, your body, and
diet culture, you will benefit from consciously sending love and
approval to your body and vowing to appreciate it exactly as it is.
Here's a ritual to help you do that. I recommend performing it
before moving on to the next chapter. All you need for this ritual
is a candle and a mister of natural rose water (any size), which
you can find online and at many health food stores.

Shower or bathe. After drying off but before dressing, sit or
stand comfortably somewhere where you won't be disturbed.
Light a candle nearby. Place one hand on your heart and one
hand on your belly. Take three deep breaths at any pace that's
comfortable for you. Then, let your breath be natural but bring
your attention to it. Notice as you breathe in and notice as you
breathe out. Notice how, as you do this, your breath naturally
begins to deepen and slow. You may notice tension in your body,
and when you do, you can simply acknowledge it, say, "Yes" to it,
and send breath to it. Just by noticing your breath, you will feel
energy begin to flow throughout your body in a healthy, nourishing way along with the breath.

During this process of breathing and acknowledging, you
may also begin to notice negative thoughts or feelings about
your body. When you do, breathe into these as well and see if you
can feel them fully and let them go. Tell yourself you don't need

them anymore. Say, silently or aloud, "I now choose to accept and approve of my body exactly as it is. I now choose to liberate it from externally imposed standards and let it be."

If you're finding it challenging to let go of these unloving thoughts and feelings, you are not alone! This is a lifetime of conditioning you are up against, and you are only just beginning to turn the tide. Instead of trying to force yourself to let go of these old feelings, you can send love and understanding to them. This will begin to unstick them and open the road for your healing.

Bring to mind all that your body does for you: it breathes your breath, moves you from place to place, digests your food, pumps your blood, purifies your organs, and helps you experience all the beauty and comfort in the world. Inwardly thank it for all these gifts. Apologize to it for any unkind thoughts or behaviors you've directed toward it, such as restricting foods or calories, ignoring its hunger cues, insulting it, or berating it.

From your heart, speak or think words to the effect of, "I am choosing now to do my best to love and approve of you exactly as you are. I am choosing to be grateful to you, to listen to you, to take wonderful care of you, and to come into harmonious alignment with you. I will probably not learn to do this instantly or perfectly, but I know that by showing up and doing my best, I will eventually succeed. I love you. Thank you for sticking with me. Thank you for being exactly as you are, and for all the gifts you've given me. Thank you, thank you, thank you."

Give yourself a hug. Then mist your entire body with the rose water to seal in your intention to align your thoughts and actions toward your body with the highest and purest vibration, which is love. Say, "Thank you, thank you, thank you. Blessed be. And so it is." Blow out the candle.

In the following days and weeks, after you shower or bathe, mist yourself with the rose water to remind yourself of your intention and to support your new habit of loving and listening to your body. Repeat after every shower or bath until the mister is empty.

Ten

SHINE LIGHT ON YOUR SHADOW

We are shaped by the values of our families and culture from our very earliest beginnings as baby humans on Earth. It's mind-boggling just how much. We learn to be nice, say thank you, and share. We learn to brush our hair, use a toilet, and chew with our mouths closed. We learn not to scream or cry when we're in public, even when we're frustrated or sad. We learn to be ashamed of our naked bodies and to publicly conceal their natural odors and functions. We learn subtle and invisible rules related to social superiorities and inferiorities, what cut of jeans is barely out of style, which feelings and qualities to publicize and which to hide, and what behavior is seen as even just a little bit weird, odd, or off.

The psychologist Erich Neumann, student of Carl Jung, wrote, "All those qualities, capacities and tendencies which do not harmonize with the collective values—everything that shuns the light of public opinion, in fact—now come together to form the shadow, that dark region of the personality which is unknown and unrecognized by the ego."[17]

Indeed, when you became socialized by your parents, family, and culture, you didn't just learn to hide certain natural tendencies, impulses, and traits from other people. In many cases, you also learned to hide them from *yourself.* Most of us don't like to think of ourselves as selfish, volatile, pushy, or cruel. We also don't want to believe ourselves to be unattractive, unintelligent, mediocre, or weak. Don't even get us started on the idea that we're uncool. Name any quality that is seen as undesirable, and chances are good you'd really prefer to believe that you're not it.

The truth is, though, that all of us possess traits that we'd rather not advertise: *lots* of them. Somewhere in the dark web of each of our personalities, all of us are mean, impatient, cranky, self-centered, snarky, and malicious. All of us have aspects that someone somewhere would call ugly, angry, dorky, frail, pathetic, and hopelessly out of touch. When we tell ourselves we're none of those things, we're lying. Lying to yourself takes a lot of energy. Keeping secrets from yourself is hard work. Perpetuating this inner charade significantly siphons off your vitality, creativity, and personal power. And anyway, who wants to be a 100 percent socially-acceptable robot? Who wants to be a constantly even-tempered, wholesome, appropriate, tasteful person who always reacts authentically-but-never-weirdly to every situation? And who is equal parts accessible and hip? You're not a Barbie doll. You're a human being!

---

17. Erich Neumann, *Depth Psychology and a New Ethic* (Boulder, CO: Shambhala, 1949), 39–40.

And human beings? We're basically very polite monkeys. We're literally primates, meaning we are 100 percent *in the monkey family*. And most of us can remember being a little monkey, who hadn't yet learned to conceal our monkey nature. Our parents or other authority figures would scold us for yelling or stomping or eating sloppily or even biting or otherwise injuring our siblings or friends. And there were times when obeying them seemed impossible, especially when other little monkeys were around. It was like we could hear the grownups telling us to stop doing what we were doing, and we maybe even *wanted* to stop doing what we were doing in order to make them happy, but somehow we still couldn't. We hadn't been successfully domesticated yet.

If you have a cat, you probably don't believe your beloved feline is "rude" when they hiss, or "bad" when they catch, injure, or even kill a mouse or a bird. When your dog humps your leg, you don't think, "You are so inappropriate—what is *wrong* with you?" If you catch a raccoon rifling through your trash, you aren't like, "That is one gross raccoon. I hope he's ashamed of himself." When a bird poops on your shoulder you don't inwardly exclaim, "What an ill-mannered bird! I hope she is really embarrassed!"

Now, I'm not suggesting that we should go around killing mice or hissing at our friends or humping legs or going through the neighbor's trash or pooping on people's shoulders. I'm just suggesting we give ourselves a break for trying to fit into this seriously complex human matrix of domestication while simultaneously being actual primates with the full range of animal instincts within us. Learning the rules of kindness, respect, and polite social behavior is one thing. Thinking of ourselves as deeply shameful and bad if we don't always naturally *want* to follow the rules every minute of every day is another. We really *are* monkeys. Our DNA is almost completely identical to other members of the monkey family. So if you're always passing judgment on yourself every time you have a disrespectful, uncool, or culturally inappropriate urge, instinct, or impulse, you're committing to an endless inner war. It's time to surrender. Lay down your weapons. Sign the primate peace treaty! You're a monkey and so is everybody else. Let's just admit it and get over it already.

To be clear: being respectful of our fellow creatures and following the golden rule are both useful policies and I fully support them! When you think about it, it's inspiring that humans have become so morally advanced that so many of us can see the immense value in behaving peacefully and treating others as we would want to be treated. I am not saying we should ignore social niceties and go around raping and rioting whenever we feel like it. I'm not saying we should strip off our clothes and run around naked whenever we feel like it. (Even though I, personally, would like nudity to be more culturally appropriate in more situations, alas: it is not. So as things currently stand, we must face the fact that nude beaches and clothing-optional hot springs aside, nudity is likely to get us fired or broken up with or arrested.)

So here's what I *am* saying. We undermine our self-respect when we expect ourselves to be *inwardly* aligned with the rules of domestication, rather than just outwardly. Being polite and appropriate is one thing. Having only polite and appropriate thoughts and desires is an entirely other thing, and not one fully functioning human being among us can legitimately claim such a thing. (And anyway, can you imagine if one of us could? Can you imagine a nonlobotomized person with absolutely zero socially unacceptable thoughts or impulses? How truly terrifying! Get that person away from me!)

My partner Ted is originally from a conservative suburb of St. Louis, Missouri. Even though he said no to being in a fraternity and said yes to starting a rock band, most of his college friends at University of Missouri were frat boys. When I met him, he looked like a dyed-in-the-wool rock dude, but I soon learned he was considered quite the weirdo among his family and friends.

I, on the other hand, grew up in the Central Valley of California. As a member of Generation X, many of the adults in my life were baby boomers who were coming of age when the hippie movement budded and blossomed. I picked up on a general assumption that the baby boomer generation and their older cultural icons, like Allen Ginsberg and Timothy Leary, were as cool as it was ever going to get. When I was in high school in the nineties, I desperately wanted to be cool, but never quite was. I was a drama geek who gazed at the skater kids across the quad at lunch and wished I possessed even a fraction of their pissed-off indifference. The best I could do was read Jack Kerouac and plaster my bedroom walls with Doors posters and fantasize about one day meeting even one person who might casually pass me a joint.

In the early years of our relationship, I moved from California to St. Louis. In those days, on the somewhat rare occasions when Ted would smoke pot, he would inevitably come back from the bathroom and admit that he had been staring in the mirror and worrying he was becoming *that guy*. "What guy?" I would ask, perplexed. "You know, that creepy, deadbeat guy with a shaggy haircut who smokes pot when he's a full-grown adult. That *weirdo*." This was so interesting to me, having grown up in a world that held up "that guy" as a cultural hero. "You don't want to be that guy? Why not? You're a musician. What musicians do you like? The Rolling Stones? Radiohead? The Cure? Don't you think they smoke the occasional joint?"

On the flip side, while I was still on my California-approved mission to be one of the cool kids, Ted would often comment on how "sweet" I was, and he didn't seem particularly impressed with my desperate efforts to be shocking, indifferent, or cutting-edge.

Our shadows are multidimensional, but in this particular example, my shadow—the part of me I desperately wanted not to admit existed—was "uncool." Ted's shadow was "a deadbeat." What was considered straitlaced in my louche California was the cultural norm in Ted's well-heeled Missouri. What Ted's domestication taught him was "that deadbeat guy," my domestication taught me was "that impossibly cool guy." The point is not that Ted's rules of domestication were right and mine were wrong, or vice versa. The point is that neither of our idealized selves were actually native to us or had anything to do with who we were. (And luckily, we were uniquely suited to help free each other from those cages.) With that in mind, we can see that we don't need to shrink ourselves to fit into the boxes our culture assigns to us, and we certainly don't need to willingly lock ourselves into them and throw away the key. But the only way we can avoid doing these things is to acknowledge the difference between our own opinions, beliefs, and preferences, and the opinions, beliefs, and preferences we've internalized from our upbringing, culture, and community.

And—once again—this is a lifelong process! Like peeling away layers of an onion, you can always uncover more of who you actually are by identifying the ideas you've internalized about who you "should" be.

There are numerous dimensions to your shadow. As you became domesticated, there were countless ways you shoved parts of yourself into the darkness with the hope they would disappear. Because these are aspects you've deemed undesirable for one reason or another, it's natural to be afraid of the very idea of investigating your shadow side. But the truth is, shadow work doesn't have to be scary. When you remember that you are, in a real sense, an exceptionally well-behaved monkey—just like every other human on Earth is a monkey—you don't have to fear any part of yourself. In fact, once you bring a shadow aspect out into the light of your awareness, that aspect can no longer sneak up on you and sabotage you. When you welcome it to the inner conference table, it offers its unique strengths and perspectives to the inner summit that is your multi-faceted personality. Best of all, it loses its status as a potentially malicious hacker, skulking around and waiting until your firewall is down so it can steal your identity and ruin your credit score.

Action Steps
• SHADOW INVESTIGATIONS •

Here are some of the fun questions that will help you explore your shadow, shine light into the darkness, and eventually welcome formerly estranged parts of you back into the fold. For best results, take notes on your initial investigations in a journal or notebook.

Who Are Your Favorite Monsters, Villains, and Antiheroes?

We may shove them to the deep dark depths of our personalities, but our shadows are certainly alive and well. As proof, consider the popularity of movies, TV shows, books, graphic novels, and documentaries featuring monsters, villains, and antiheroes whom we either love, loathe, or otherwise can't look away from. In many cases, this is because they represent one or more of our shadow aspects: something within us that we don't want to look at or claim. Watching them or reading about them allows our shadows to live vicariously, and—just for a fleeting moment—to feel seen, heard, and allowed out of the cage.

First, let's talk about creatures. Do you have a certain mythological monster that particularly calls to you? For a lifelong friend of mine, it's zombies: he can't get enough of those apocalyptic survival stories, especially when zombies are involved. For me, it's vampires. Though it's not my favorite thing to admit it, I couldn't put the *Twilight* books down. And as for *Buffy the Vampire Slayer?* Once I watched the first episode, the rest of my life took a back seat until I'd devoured every episode of the series. It was as if it was my sole function in life to binge-watch *Buffy*. You may or may not have such a fascination. If you do, though, it would be a good place to start when investigating what this might have to tell you about your shadow side. And if you think you don't, take an extra moment to think it over. I didn't realize the vampire thread (as obvious as it was) until I was quizzing my old friend about his love of zombies and he asked, "Okay, now what's the deal with you and vampires?"

If you really think about zombies and vampires, you can see what our fascinations may be trying to tell us. You can perform a similar analysis on your own monster movie obsession.

Zombies have no wills or personalities of their own. If you can't get enough of those zombie stories, are you afraid of giving up your own preferences, opinions, and choices to your culture, community, or career? Is it possible you feel your young, idealistic self slipping away as you daily show up at your current workplace? Or, are you afraid that somewhere deep inside, you long to steal the free will of others, perhaps by being a tyrant, dictator, or megalomaniac? Or maybe both? (Remember, this doesn't have to be scary when you remember that your shadow side is only part of who you are and acknowledging it doesn't mean it will take over your life.)

Vampires literally can't live unless they sap away the life force of others, resulting in their victims' deaths or their transformations into becoming vampires themselves. Vampirism is in many ways similar to modern capitalism. Every time we buy a plastic bottle or take a ride in a car, we are harming our planet. When we take a bite of non-free trade chocolate, we are supporting slave labor. When we blithely purchase sweatshop clothing or chintzy décor, we are basically doing both. Is it possible that you fear being a vampire? Have you been projecting your judgment about the harmful effects of capitalism, rather than fully owning that you contribute to those effects yourself? If so, might you be able to forgive yourself for participating in the world you were born into, while still taking action to change things as you feel guided?

Whatever monsters or creatures you're most attracted to (if any), explore your feelings about them in your journal. Here are some journaling prompts to get you started:

- What scares you most about this being?

- What fascinates you about them?

- What societal horrors might they metaphorically represent (like vampires representing capitalism or zombies representing becoming a cog in a corporate machine)?

- Are there any qualities they possess that you are terrified of possessing yourself, or that you haven't wanted to admit to yourself for any reason?

- Might you be able to lovingly forgive yourself if you do possess them in some small way?

- Can you imagine ways in which it might be fun to let yourself embody these qualities, or at least acknowledge and claim them? (Without, of course, harming yourself or anyone else?)
- Can you think of ways you might safely express these qualities, perhaps through art or some form of play?

Next, look at individual "bad guy" characters or even notorious historical figures you are drawn to or fascinated by, such as the Joker, Darth Vader, Cruella DeVille, serial killer Charles Manson, or cult leader Anne Hamilton-Byrne. In some cases, you might hate to love them, in others you might love to hate them, and in still others you might not love *or* hate them, but still somehow feel inexplicably drawn to learn and think about them. The important thing is that they thrill or fascinate you in some way. Once you've made a list, explore each one in your journal using the same journaling prompts from above.

Finally, list and similarly investigate characters or people you're drawn to who are perhaps not all bad, but definitely not all good either. Characters on this list might include Walter White from *Breaking Bad*, Melisandre from *Game of Thrones*, or Spike from *Buffy the Vampire Slayer*. Historical figures might include problematic, multidimensional people such as former US President Richard Nixon, double agent Kim Philby, and Queen Didda of Kashmir.

Who Drives You Crazy or Makes You Angry?

Next, let's look at those people who irritate, annoy, and infuriate you. This list can include friends, family, coworkers, neighbors, and acquaintances, as well as people with whom you're familiar but don't know personally, such as political figures and entertainment personalities. In some cases, the behavior that bothers you will be obvious, and your feelings will be easily justified. In other cases, your negative feelings will be more mysterious. Perhaps one of the people on your list is beloved by many, but for whatever reason you just happen to be bothered every time you see them on television, or someone brings them up in conversation. Who are these people? Make a list.

Be sure only to include people who *actually* irritate or anger you, not just people who you think *should* irritate or anger you. It's interesting to consider that there are plenty of people doing egregious, unconscionable things in the world, from dictators to terrorists to owners of businesses that cruelly exploit people and the environment. But it's likely that very few of these people actually frustrate you or cause you to crave a shot of Jägermeister before ten in the morning. And some of the people who *do* affect you this way aren't even doing anything that bad: maybe it's just a tone of voice they use that bugs you, or their consistently incorrect grammar, or the way they're always checking their phone, or their dandruff, or their self-satisfied smile. (I know for me, if I witness someone playing air guitar while listening to a song they like—even for a second—it's highly likely they'll find their way onto this list. I know it sounds harsh, but there's nothing to be done. I didn't *choose* to hate casual air guitar. I was born this way.)

Keep writing until you've listed everyone you can think of who bugs or enrages you, whether or not you can put your finger on *why*. Even include types that tend to bug you, such as people who don't match their belt to their shoes, smokers, or members of a particular religious group or political party. Then, take a moment with each one and ask yourself the following questions. Answer them in your journal.

- Can you describe what it is about this person (or type of person) that bothers you?
- If you can't describe it exactly, do your best to describe the annoying feeling as you experience it.
- What is wrong with this person, in your opinion?
- What would need to change about this person in order for them to stop bothering you?
- What quality or behavior of theirs do you never want to experience or witness, ever again?

After you've answered these questions for each person, go back through and deeply consider your answers. See if you can identify any shadow aspects of your own personality that each person is mirroring back to you. Because here's the thing: there's a reason why some people make you cringe, grit your teeth, or ball your hands into fists while others don't really make you feel one way or another. Often, that reason is related to one or more of your own unwanted or unclaimed shadow aspects that person is mirroring back to you. I'm not implying that you're a veritable clone of anyone on your list. For example, if one of these people is a world leader who is making policy changes that hurt children and destroy the environment, I'm not implying that you are a closeted asshole and that you secretly want to let greed and power take over your life. I'm also not saying that once you do some shadow work, the people on your list won't (or shouldn't) bug you ever again.

As I've said before, we become more whole, empowered, and at peace when we uncover previously unclaimed aspects of ourselves: when we admit them, listen to them, and even begin to give them a seat at the table. When you stop shoving them into the cold, freaky basement of your consciousness, they will no longer have the ability to rise up from the depths and wreak havoc in your life. And when other more palatable aspects of your personality keep them in check (as can happen once you bring your shadow out into the open), these previously closeted aspects can even offer useful wisdom and perspectives on occasion, and generally make you a more grounded and well-rounded person.

So, with all this in mind, as you look at what you've previously written for each person on your list, ask yourself:

- Can I admit any similarities I might have to this person (or type of person), now or in the past?

- Would it sometimes be fun to embody any of their traits that annoy or anger me?

- What would it feel like (hypothetically) if I sometimes let myself be annoying in exactly this way? Might it sometimes feel good?'

- In what healthy, balanced, non-harmful ways might I begin to employ some of these personality traits in my life?

- If I realize I might be similar to this person or group in some ways, or that I may have been in the past, can I forgive myself for these traits? Can I claim them and let them be a part of the multi-faceted being that is (or was) me? Or, can I compassionately see how I might have developed these traits out of pain, loneliness, fear, or despair?

- Is there an action I can take that will help me feel more empowered around this person, or in relation to this person? (For example, by standing up for yourself or for

> a cause you care about that is in symbolic opposition
> to what this person represents to you, or by drawing a
> boundary with a family member or coworker?)

Not all of these questions will apply to every person or type of person on your list, but at least one of them should give you some degree of clarity in each instance and help you to bring your shadow aspects out into the light of day. Don't feel limited by these questions: if you feel guided to go in a different direction with your investigations, feel free. No one knows you like you do.

Our shadow sides are not always filled with traits that are negative in our own eyes or in the eyes of the world. In some cases, when someone annoys you and you don't exactly know why (or even if you do), it's because there's a positive aspect of them that you haven't fully claimed for yourself. We don't always want to admit when we're jealous or envious, because those are feelings we judge or just don't want to claim. Which means jealousy and envy, when we acknowledge them and bring them out in the open, can point the way to *positive* aspects, talents, behaviors, and traits that we've been keeping in the shadows. Which brings us to ...

Who Inspires Your Jealousy and Envy?

Jealousy and envy on their own can often be shadow aspects, because they are not feelings many of us want to own up to. By admitting to ourselves that we feel bitter or negative about another's success, we are admitting that we believe they are better or more fortunate than us in some way. This—we think—will just add insult to injury. So often when we hide our feelings in the darkness of our shadow, it's because we think we'll have to keep feeling them forever. But nothing could be further from the truth.

Actually, noticing our jealousy or envy, and allowing it, is a way of bringing our positive, empowered, desirable shadow aspects into the light, and beginning to embody those aspects. Because more often than not, when you're jealous or envious of someone, it's because you're ignoring a cherished goal or refusing to claim a positive quality or natural strength. When you think of jealousy and envy not as life sentences but as X's that mark the spot where treasure is buried in your personality, they often clear right up as soon as that treasure is acknowledged and owned. That's why when I notice jealousy or envy now, I get excited, like, "Oh, what's that about? What hidden parts of me are asking to be seen?"

This will make more sense when you try the following exercise. Make a list of everyone you're the least bit jealous or envious of. After you've written down any obvious contenders, consider if anyone from your previous list (of people who annoy or anger you) might fit the bill. Get really honest with yourself and pay especial attention to anyone on the list who irritates you for a reason that isn't entirely clear to you, or who bugs you because of a positive quality rather than a negative one. If it's a person lots of people love but you can't stand, this would be a clue that they might belong on this list.

For example, in the past I have been disproportionately annoyed by Neil DeGrasse Tyson, Dave Grohl, and Neil Gaiman. Positive comments about these people and their work (and there are many!) only served to further inflame my irritation. It later became clear to me that I was envious of their confidence in their own uniqueness, and jealous that they were so beloved for that very quality. I thought, "Who are *they* to be so comfortable in their own skin, and so blissfully self-assured?" But the real question, I realized, is "Who am I *not* to be?"

Another time I did this exercise, I discovered that everyone on my list was a video blogger. Then it dawned on me that—*hello!*—I wanted to start making YouTube videos! Once I did, my envy toward these people quickly faded. I didn't need to be as wildly successful as they were for it to fade, either. I just had to take action on something that was important to me.

Once you've written your own list of people whom you are (or may be) jealous or envious of, take a moment to see if there are any common threads in your list. Like Neil, Dave, and Neil, do they all seem to behave as if they are entitled to be universally beloved? Or, do any of them share a certain skill or form of artistic expression like the video bloggers on my list? If so, look deeply within yourself to see if these are qualities or activities that you'd like to embody or try. Then, brainstorm some ways you can immediately begin to do so.

Author Marianne Williamson wrote, "Our deepest fear is not that we are inadequate. Our deepest fear is that we are powerful beyond measure. It is our light, not our darkness that most frightens us. We ask ourselves, Who am I to be brilliant, gorgeous, talented, and fabulous? Actually, who are you not to be? You are a child of God. Your playing small does not serve the world."[18]

No doubt, during your investigations in this chapter, you uncovered qualities in yourself that are desirable in the eyes of the world and qualities that are undesirable in the eyes of the world. Remember that everyone is a full-spectrum being: not just you. We can all be greedy, mean, and obtuse, just as we can all be gen-

---

18. Marianne Williamson, *A Return to Love: Reflections on the Principles of A Course in Miracles* (New York: HarperPerennial, 1992), 190–91.

erous, loving, and brilliant. We all have strengths and we all have weaknesses. None of it matters when it comes to loving yourself, just as none of it matters when it comes to loving your child, your brother, or your cat. You love them not because of traits they do or do not have but because of their beautiful essence: the part of them that transcends all value judgments and worldly concerns. You can love yourself in exactly the same way now.

The value of investigating your shadow is that it's a way of expressing love to yourself by letting yourself embody the fullness of who you are in this lifetime. Remember: uncovering your shadow is a lifelong pursuit.

Place one hand on your belly and one hand on your heart. Take a few deep, conscious breaths. Then, lovingly commit to a lifetime of consciously investigating the parts of yourself that have previously been hidden in the shadows. When you do this, you will be repeatedly astounded to discover that you are much more precious, exceptional, and filled with light than you could have ever suspected.

Eleven
FEEL, HEAL, AND BE FREE

Have you ever experienced the death of a loved one? I've lost several loved ones over the course of my life, including beloved friends and family members who were human, feline, and canine. If you've also had this experience, you know that once someone you love is on the other side, it becomes crystal clear that they were—in the truest sense—absolutely perfect. The things you thought of as their imperfections were actually only temporary and weren't even who they really were. Their neutral and positive traits also weren't why you loved them, although you loved many of those traits. Even your favorite and most treasured expressions of your deceased loved one's personality were just temporary, surface emanations of something that ran much deeper. What you really loved about them—and love about them still—is eternal. It's not something you can describe, but it *is* something you unmistakably feel and know. When you bring their face to mind (or their laugh, or the joyful wag of their tail, or the feel of their furry, purring body on your lap), you connect with that ineffable, transcendent, timeless essence of what is so dear to you about them, even now. It's as evocative as the memory of a crackling campfire or the scent of rain on pavement.

In just the same way, you're not your traits. You're not your shadow side *or* the side you show the world. You're not your body and you're also not your mind. You're not your age, your nationality, your gender, your hair color, or your size. You're not the world's perception of you, and you're not even your own perception of yourself. As I described in chapter two, these things are all just clouds, passing through the sky that is you. Throughout your life, your traits and your relationship with your traits will shift and shuffle around and even—eventually, in all cases—dissolve away into the nothingness from which they came. But *you* won't go anywhere.

To reiterate: you—your true self, who you really are—are not the temporary appearance of clouds. You're the eternal, unbounded, unchanging presence of the sky. Just like your loved ones, Infinity is your identity. You're one with the power that creates and sustains the planet, the galaxy, the solar system, and the Universe.

True healing comes from repeatedly remembering this truth and continually cultivating an awareness of it. When you do this (and you're dabbling in it right now just by reading and considering these words), you'll clearly see that any mistakes you've made, or might make, or will make in the future—as well as any traits you perceive as less than perfect in any way—are not only not who you are, they're also not actually real. (Neither, for that matter, are the traits you consider positive and worthy of approval.)

They're illusions. And so they need not hold you back from loving yourself fully, right now, and letting go of anything standing in the way of your joy.

Yes, there is a relative reality to everything you're experiencing in this temporary little existence we call your life. There's a level of perception from which we can—for example—make choices that heal the planet and choices that harm it or engage in behavior that hurts other people or helps them. As we learn what our souls came here to learn, we can certainly make what you might call "mistakes" along the way, and those mistakes can be helpful and necessary learning tools. With this in mind, it makes sense to do our best to be kind and loving, and to engage in behavior that heals rather than harms, even though we know none of us will ever do this perfectly.

Despite the brief and illusory nature of this thing we call life, we will still take pleasure in a new coat or a manicure or a compliment, and we will still be bummed out if a haircut doesn't look like we thought it would. In other words, we needn't deny that we're having a temporary human experience. But when we forget what is *really* going on, we can get so caught up in the ups and downs that we lose sight of the true reality, which is where sanity and happiness live. It's also the place we can go to heal ourselves deeply and become even freer than we were before.

Take a moment to consider what eternity actually means: beyond the appearance of time and space. Here, beyond the illusion of limitation, you're not a flawed, temporary being who makes mistakes and hurts other people or the planet, or has bad hair days, or needs mascara in order to feel presentable. Rather, you're a point of perfection, emanating out in all directions forever. Just as the sky underlies the fleeting appearance of clouds, this—your true identity—underlies the fleeting appearance of

your seeming imperfections and struggles (and all other temporary traits) in this lifetime.

That's why beating yourself up for perceived mistakes or
imperfections makes no sense. Criticizing yourself mercilessly
or harping on seeming failures does nothing but hold you back
from being who you are, and helping others to be who they are,
and transforming the world in a positive way. Because if you
want to create positive change in the world, the very best place
to start is by loving yourself, having compassionate for yourself,
and grounding yourself in an abiding sense of calm inner peace.

Still, in this life experience, we will on occasion beat ourselves
up. I had a bit of an unkind inner monologue just yesterday. I
don't mean to imply that if you ever criticize yourself, it means
you've failed. It just means you're human! But we can practice
putting self-blame and self-criticism in perspective when we do
engage in it, and we can stop identifying with it, so that we don't
feel defined or ruled by it. This way, we dim the harsh fluorescent
lighting of our negative self-talk and learn to see ourselves in a
much more flattering light. Learning to do this is the subject of
this chapter.

Peace is one of those words we've heard so much, we tend to
gloss over it. So think about the quality of peace for a moment.
Find it within you. It's here, right now: in this moment. It's underneath and around and within everything else you seem to be
experiencing. It's *always* right here.

Of course, there will be times when your sense of inner peace
appears to be disrupted or temporarily out of reach, just as the
surface of an alpine lake can seem to be disturbed by wind or
rain or a child skipping a stone, even though it's always just as
peaceful at its depths. But you can cultivate habits that help you
regularly restore your serenity by diving into the inner peace that

resides within you and around you, always. Practices such as meditating, going out in nature, consciously releasing old beliefs and emotions that are holding you back, and engaging in mindful self-care rituals will help you anchor yourself in peace again and again, so that even if you lose sight of it for a moment (and you will), you learn to know and trust that it's still there.

You might have picked up the idea that spiritual practices such as meditation and mindfulness will take forever: that you have to struggle and practice and sit through boredom and uncomfortable sitting positions, and then repeat this process regularly for weeks or months or even years before you experience results. But that's not actually the case. The truth is that every time you choose to proactively heal yourself and connect with the serene and eternal essence of who you really are, you will succeed. Sure, sometimes your spiritual efforts will yield more profound experiences than other times. Sometimes you'll feel ecstatic and sometimes you'll feel just slightly less annoyed. Sometimes your spiritual practice will be a multi-course farm-to-table brunch and sometimes it will be a quick granola bar between meetings to keep your blood sugar from dropping too low. Regardless of what you do and how you experience it, if you show up with the intention to connect with the eternal truth of who you are, you'll nourish and fortify your spirit and your soul.

Action Step
• BE INFINITY •

In chapter 2, you practiced stepping out of your ego and into the truth of who you are, which is infinite. In chapter 7, you practiced centering yourself and grounding your energy. Now you're going to do both these things at once, while adding a new perspective into the mix. When you have ten to twenty minutes where you can sit quietly without being disturbed (perhaps in front of your altar with a candle burning, but this is not necessary), perform the following exercise:

Begin by sitting comfortably, with your spine relatively straight in a comfortable way. Take three deep, conscious breaths at a pace that feels comfortable to you. For each of these three breaths, make your exhale audible as if you are fogging up a window. You can do this with your mouth open or closed. Then allow your breath to become natural but keep your attention on it. Notice as you breathe in and notice as you breathe out. Also notice that as you do this, your breath naturally begins to deepen, and your body naturally begins to relax. See if you can become sensitized to the way breath moves energy throughout your body and brings consciousness to tense areas, which then allows them to relax as if they are being massaged by the breath. Continue with this conscious breathing for a few minutes. When your mind wanders (and it will!) there's no need to judge or scold yourself: simply bring your attention right back to the breath.

When you feel relaxed and centered, bring your awareness to the earth beneath you. Do your best to consider its magnitude and scope. Think of the billions of humans, and also the diversity of landscapes, and the vast abundance of trees, animals, micro-organisms, rocks, plants, water, air, and grains of sand. See your-self—your body, mind, and spirit—as one with all of these things: interconnected in a vast network of energy and consciousness.

Now bring your awareness back to the breath for a few inhales and exhales, once again paying close attention to when you are breathing in and when you're breathing out, as well as the sensa-tions in your body that go along with the breath.

Place your awareness now on the atmosphere of the earth. Send your awareness up and out of the earth's atmosphere, into space. Imagine the moon orbiting the earth, and then the other planets in our solar system, as well as the sun. Expand yourself to be one with the solar system. In truth, you are not separate. When you conceptualize something, it's accurate to say that it's wholly encompassed within your mind, and therefore within your being. And at the same time the solar system is within you, you are within it. Observe both these perspectives simultaneously. Feel your oneness with the solar system.

Once again, attend to your breath: inhale, exhale, and bring your mind, body, and spirit into even greater harmony as you breathe.

Expand your awareness to the galaxy, and then the Universe: the vast, expansive, infinite reality of All That Is. As you hold this within your mind as best you can, feel the Universe within you, and also know that you are within it. When this feels palpable to you, see if you can bring to mind any of your temporary human problems. Take a moment to observe how small that problem is in the entire scope of things, while still having compassion for yourself for experiencing it. Breathe in: feel the problem. Breathe out: notice how much space is around the problem. Breathe in: think of anything you're worried about. Breathe out: notice how much space is around that worry. Let the exhale be a way of releasing your identification or ownership of any worry or problem you bring to mind. Begin to think "Allow" on the inhale and "Release" on the exhale. As you release, feel the energy of your problem melting and transforming as you hand it over to Infinity.

Repeat this process until you feel centered and calm.

When you forget or temporarily lose sight of the fact that you're one with Infinity—that you are within it and it is within you—your worries and problems take up a disproportionate amount of space in your identity and consciousness. But when you put your worries in perspective, it becomes easier to release attachment to them. They may still be there, but you will not be grasping at them anymore, or believing it's important to hold onto them. This allows the Universe—again, with whom you are one—to swoop in and take them off your hands, healing and dissolving them, and ultimately transmuting them into blessings and beauty. In the next section, we'll explore this dynamic in greater detail.

Relax, Allow, and Receive

Many years ago, I decided to launch a one-woman feng shui consulting business in Los Angeles, where I lived at the time. I had recently graduated from the Western School of Feng Shui Practitioner Training Program. I had a website. I had brochures and business cards. I was going to weird networking meetings in business attire. I was doing my very best to get the word out with the resources I had. But I hadn't had much success. My consultations were painfully few and far between. After constantly working at least one job at a time to maintain a steady (if not large) income since the age of eighteen, I was sort of freaking out. Also, I was berating myself with an internal monologue that went something like, "What kind of feng shui consultant am I if I can't even attract abundance in my *own* life? No wonder no one is hiring me! I'm a fake."

While I was in the midst of what had slowly but surely become a sort of mental water torture, a good friend came to visit me in Venice Beach from her home in St. Louis, Missouri. I don't remember how I heard about it or why I decided it was a good idea, but the first day she was in town, I took her to an interesting event: Mother Meera offering darshan (this is a Hindi word that means being in the presence of a holy being) at UCLA. According to Mother Meera's website, she "is an embodiment of the Divine Feminine, the Divine Mother on earth." While she is originally from India and now lives in Germany, she tours the world offering darshan. In Mother Meera's case, darshan involves sitting on a stage in silence transmitting the presence of the Divine Mother.

Well, there we sat: on folding chairs in a large auditorium, our flip phones fully powered off in our purses. On the stage, Mother Meera also sat, gazing out at everyone with equanimity and love. The whole theater was in total silence. But even before that silence began, my mind was babbling belligerently. "Why did I bring my friend here?" I thought. "She probably thinks this is the most bizarre thing ever. She's straight off the plane from the Midwest, and I take her to *this*? What's my problem? Way to downplay the California stereotype. And I can't even say anything to her! I can't even apologize or explain or make a joke about it! How embarrassing. I could just die." And then my self-nagging monologue would come back around to something like, "I'd seriously better make some money soon. I can't believe I thought I could pull off a feng shui business in Los Angeles. My business cards aren't right. But it's not like anyone's looking at them anyway. Some feng shui consultant I am. Ugh." (And on and on.) My stomach was in knots. I could feel a headache coming on. I couldn't *wait* for the damn darshan to end.

... And then! A simple message slipped into my consciousness like a golden envelope: "What if it's all okay? What if it's not *just okay*, what if it's all perfect?" It wasn't just words appearing in my mind, either. It was a feeling. It was a sense. It was a *knowing*, even. And it wasn't linear, like words on a page: it expanded out in all directions like a thousand-petaled lotus. It was beautiful. "It's all there anyway," it seemed to say in not so many words, "so you might as well accept it, embrace it, and love it. Exactly as it is, right this moment. *Right now*. What if you just said to yourself, 'I can release all worry and resistance because this is exactly where I'm meant to be.'" This thought/feeling/perception/multi-dimensional knowing quickly morphed into elation and relief. After so many months of berating myself and berating reality, the boulder that had been my heart suddenly felt like a flock of seagulls. I smiled and relaxed into my seat, content with myself and the moment, and finally (finally!) at peace in my mind.

I cannot stress enough what a miracle this was. It was such a departure from where I had been mentally! I could never have predicted such a rapid 180. Was it because of Mother Meera's purportedly Divine Presence, said to dissolve blocks and open your being to Infinity? Um … *maybe*? I can't say for sure, but I tend to think that had something to do with it.

As my friend and I spilled out of the auditorium and into the early evening sun, I felt like I'd been soaking in a hot spring for hours. As we walked, I rooted around in my purse and turned my phone back on. Instantly, it alerted me that I had four missed calls. All of them were related to my feng shui business: three were requests for consultations and one was an inquiry from a local radio show that was looking for feng shui consultants to interview.

After months and months of almost zero interest in my feng shui business, I received *four phone calls* in the two hours I was in the auditorium with Mother Meera.

Some people might say, "Mother Meera is a miracle worker! She drew abundance and success into your life." And in a way, I might agree. And, the actual, nuts-and-bolts dynamic at work as

I perceived it was this: I had been in complete resistance to what was happening. I was at war with the present moment. I thought nothing was unfolding as it should be, and I had to fix it all with the power of my own mind. As soon as that resistance lifted (which may or may not have had something to do with Mother Meera precisely, but as I said, I tend to think it did), I became receptive, and Universal support came rushing in. The Universe *wanted* to support me! It was just waiting for me to let my guard down. It was like the Universe was saying, "Can I help you move that sofa?" And I was like, "No, I got it, I got it, don't worry about it, I got it," and as soon as I stopped trying to move it on my own and just completely dropped it, the Universe sent in a team of angels to move it for me.

While this is sort of a highly concentrated example, we are all usually experiencing this dynamic in some capacity throughout our lifetimes. Anytime you feel internally resistant to something, or in opposition to something—anything—you are holding the Universe back from helping and restricting the natural flow of blessings and divine support that's always knocking, waiting for you to open the door so it can come rushing in. But experiencing resistance is a natural part of being human. That's why it's so helpful to cultivate an awareness of resistance and a habit of effectively letting it go. This is a lifelong practice, and it's best to think of it that way: we're not striving to get to a static point of permanent perfection. We're just showing up again and again, noticing where we're holding onto something or pushing something away, and then doing our best to let it go.

Feel and Heal

When I was sitting next to my friend in that auditorium with Mother Meera on the stage and my mind going crazy, the problem was not that I was thinking thoughts that were making me feel uncomfortable. The problem was that I was fighting both the thoughts and the feelings they brought up. I was also so identified with my stream of thought and the inner war with my feelings, they began to seem like my only reality: I mistook them for who I was. That made them almost impossible to let go of. It was like I was both a boxer and that same boxer's opponent, mistakenly believing that the boxing ring in which I was fighting with myself was my entire identity and world.

The miracle happened not when one side of my consciousness knocked the other side out cold, but when I let go of the outcome of what happening in the ring. Once I stopped identifying with them, the fighting factions within me began to lose steam, and eventually gave up the match altogether. One of them threw his arm around the other, and they left the building to go have a beer.

Even if you're not having an acute inner conflict like I was at that time, if you're like most of us, you're probably experiencing similar resistance in one or more life areas. Human minds are funny. They run all over the place and tell us all kinds of conflicting things. They pick fights with themselves. They get bent out of shape, obsessive, afraid, frustrated, and bored. In turn, all kinds of emotions get activated based on the way our minds interpret the world. That's just what they do, and we can't really stop this dynamic. But we *can* learn to step out of the boxing ring of resistance so we can create space around our thoughts and let our feelings flow. When we do that, the frenetic nature of them dissipates and they slowly unravel and fade. This opens us up to the present moment, which is where all our joy, inspiration, and intuition live. Letting our feelings flow and creating space around our thoughts is what allows us to connect deeply with other people and ourselves. Stepping out of the boxing ring opens us up to Infinity: we are no longer roped into a tiny square designated for repetitive conflict. We are free.

Right now, with the following exercise, you can practice stepping out of the boxing ring in any and all life areas in which you currently feel limited, frustrated, or stuck.

Action Step
• ESTABLISH PEACE WITHIN •

In your journal, make a list of life areas in which you are experiencing any sort of internal conflict, as well as life areas in which you would like to move forward, transform, heal, or evolve. You don't have to write these in any particular way at this point: just make a note or bullet point that clearly describes each challenge, goal, or desire. Keep writing until you can't think of anything else you want to heal, manifest, or change. (You can always repeat this exercise later, though, so don't worry about forgetting something.)

Now, with each item you've listed, rephrase it so it's a positive statement describing how you want to feel or what you want to experience, but state it in the present tense as if it's already true. So bridge the "want" energy by bringing it into present-moment phrasing. This in itself is a powerful way to attune to the frequency of the desire so you can begin attracting it immediately.

So, for example:

- "I'm anxious so much of the time," could be transformed into, "My mind is calm, clear, and serene."

- "I want to make more money," could be rewritten as, "I always have plenty of money."

- "I worry people don't like me," could become, "I am loved and lovable, liked and likable."

Once you've translated everything on your list to a positive affirmation as demonstrated above, do the following meditation. There's no need to memorize this before you begin; you can refer to the instructions throughout the process:

Light a candle on your self-love altar and sit comfortably in front of it with your spine straight in a relaxed way. As you did in the meditation exercise above, breathe in deeply and breathe out fully three times. Then allow your breath to be natural but place your attention on it for several more breaths. Notice as you breathe in and notice as you breathe out. Notice that as you do this, your breath naturally begins to deepen and the tension in your body naturally begins to relax. If your mind wanders during this process, smile gently to your mind and lovingly bring it back to the breath. Remember: this is just what minds do, so there's absolutely no reason to judge yourself.

Bring your awareness now to the first positive affirmation statement on your list. Breathe in that positive statement. Then breathe it out. Then allow yourself to feel any feelings that are not in alignment with that statement. So, for example, let's say you're working with the statement, "My mind is calm, clear, and serene." When you say or think that statement to yourself, and search your consciousness for thoughts or feelings that don't match that statement, you might begin to feel worried about money, or whether your partner loves you enough, or you might see pictures of unlucky occurrences that might befall you in the future. When this happens, welcome the feeling instead of fighting it. Start with the first one that arises: let's say it's worry about money. Breathe in and feel the worry completely: really let yourself stress. Then, as you breathe out, choose to let the stress go. Think, "What if I just let that feeling go? How would it feel?" Then imagine you're breathing that worry out and letting it go completely. If it helps, you might imagine the worry like black smoke in your aura (or personal energy field), and as you exhale, you blow it out and it dissolves into light. Or, it might be more helpful to imagine the worry like something you're hanging onto for dear life, and as you exhale, you release it and let it fall over a bridge and into a river below. (You'll discover what works best for you.)

Continue with each feeling until it dissipates. If you're having trouble letting it go, you can let go of wanting to let it go. Then see if it becomes easier to actually let it go. When you've released this feeling as much as you can, imagine your entire body filled with golden-white light. Breathe in that light and let it replace stress with comfort, tension with relaxation. Imagine the light repairing and restructuring any holes or injuries in your energetic field.

Once this feels complete with the first item on your list, move on to the next. You may want to work with two or three items at a time and then take a break and come back until you've worked your way through everything on your list. Remember to refill your aura with golden-white light each time so you aren't just releasing vibrations that aren't in alignment with you, but also healing, repairing, and restructuring in order to create permanent changes in your energetic field.

· · · · · · · · · ·

Throughout your day, even when you're not sitting in front of your self-love altar, when any sort of negative feeling arises, you can work through a similar process. For example, maybe you're looking at Instagram and suddenly you realize you feel vaguely unsettled. In the past, you may have tried to avoid that feeling by distracting yourself with something else. This time, I suggest that you welcome it and even get curious about it. Take a deep, conscious breath and feel that discomfort, even if you still don't understand its source. Really go into the center of it. It's likely that you'll gain insight into its origin at this point, like, "Oh, I began feeling this way because I saw that my friend just got a new car and it activated my worry about money and also a feeling of envy." Then you can go into the worry and the envy in turn, breathing in, feeling it, and breathing out as you let it go. Continue with each one until the feeling dissipates, and then breathe in the golden-white light, letting it recharge and restructure your energy field.

The allowing part of this practice is where you stop the war with yourself. The letting-go process is when you step out of identification with your ego, or the part of you that's narrating the story of your life as you perceive it. The letting-go is also when you move the emotions out of your body and the limiting thoughts out of your mind—because neither of them is you: they're just passing *through* you. When you allow them fully, and then immediately set the intention to let them go, they naturally dissipate like low-hanging clouds in sunshine and a brisk wind. Synchronizing this process with your breath organically helps this process along. So does calling in the light. Once you step out of the war within, allow your feelings, and come into harmony with yourself and the present moment, you might naturally think to yourself (like I did during the darshan), "What if it's all perfect? What if I'm, actually, in exactly the right place at the right time? What if it's all unfolding in the most ideal possible way?"

This process won't be perfect, but when you set the intentions to first allow and then let go, you'll definitely get stuck feelings moving, which will make a hugely positive difference. So don't aim for perfection, just progress.

After just a week or two of consistently reminding yourself to feel, heal, and let go, it will start to become a habit, and you'll become much less likely to get carried away by negative thoughts, feelings, beliefs, and expectations. This habit will easily catch because its benefits are immediate and immense. Right away, you'll feel lighter, happier, and freer. And more and more frequently, you'll begin to naturally magnetize positive conditions, just like all those phone calls I received during the Mother Meera event. Why? Because you'll no longer be resisting your natural flow of blessings and success.

"Wait," you might be thinking. "*What* natural flow of blessings and success? Is that a thing? I thought life was a struggle. I didn't think the Universe owed me blessings. Did I miss something?" Actually, your natural state is one of ease and flow. The Universe *wants* to bestow gifts upon you. You are *naturally* rich and successful, loved and lovable. How do I know? I don't actually. But what I do know is that our lives take on a shape according to the stories we tell ourselves. We make choices and take action according to those stories, and then they actually become true for us. So you can believe that life is a struggle, or you can believe that life is waiting for you to get out of the way so it can bless you with every wonderful thing. You're going to tell yourself one story or another, so why not tell yourself one that empowers you?

In this story of endlessly flowing blessings, you don't need to *add* anything. You just need to *subtract* resistance to the present moment: you just need to come into harmony with what is. From there, innate guidance and inspiration will, at various times and in various ways, propel you to take action. But that action will not feel strenuous or forced. Rather, it will be as if you are carried along buoyantly in the clear, sparkling river of your own joy.

But don't take my word for it. Try feeling and releasing as described above while believing that a constant flow of blessings is your birthright and your natural state. Do it in front of your altar and any time you notice a challenging feeling come up throughout the day. Stay with this practice every day for one week. And see what happens.

Twelve

HOW TO BE A RAINBOW

Do you understand rainbows? I don't. Try as I might, the actual dynamics of light bending or refracting to form a luminescent ribbon of all the visual colors of the spectrum is not something I've ever come close to getting my head around.

But whether I understand it or not, the fact remains that *something* happens so that water droplets make it so the light of the sun bends in a way that allows our eyes to temporarily see each color in its purest form. It's still the same light. It doesn't actually separate and become its own thing... Only it *does*. Where there was once nothing but sky, something arises that our eyes see, and our minds conceptualize as a singular, radiant, and miraculous object: a rainbow.

When you think of it this way, can you see how *you* are also a rainbow? You are not separate from the light of spirit, just as your form is not separate from your invisible essence. Neither is your form separate from your ancestors or your relatives or your descendants—how could it be? Furthermore, without this planet, this solar system, this galaxy, or this Universe, you would not be. You evolved here and your body is formed out of the materials that also create the earth, the sky, and the stars. You breathe the oxygen of this atmosphere. You're sustained by the food that grows from the soil. Even though you temporarily appear as a singular being, you are even more truly one with everything and an emanation of everything: visible and invisible, known and unknown, air and fire and water and earth and spirit. Like a rainbow, your appearance is fleeting but your essence is eternal. You are Infinity refracted, creating the radiant and impossibly beautiful appearance of you.

Obviously, this is a metaphor. And no metaphor is perfect but it's a pretty good one. And, astonishingly, this metaphor has a practical application in both ancient and modern holistic healing modalities. Every major color of the rainbow resonates at a point in your aura or energetic field. You may have heard of this body of wisdom before. It's called your chakra system: an invisible energetic framework that's utilized by Ayurvedic practitioners, acupuncturists, yogis, Reiki healers, massage therapists, sound healers, and plenty of other metaphysically-minded people and holistic healing practitioners.

If you're brand-new to the concept of chakras, this chapter will orient you to what chakras are, where they reside in your energetic body, what they represent, and how sensing them can help you heal yourself on every level and love yourself more than ever before. But whether you're a chakra novice, a chakra expert, or anywhere in between, you're going to get something out of reading this chapter. The chakra system is one of those epic topics that continually open up to us and offer us fresh wisdom and perspective throughout our lifetimes. Even if you've heard or read something about chakras before, when you read it again or hear it presented in a slightly different way, you have the opportunity to integrate it on a deeper level, and to step even more fully into the healing and empowerment it offers.

Your chakra system is the alchemy of your spirit and the energetic infrastructure of your emotional well-being. Through your thoughts, feelings, intentions, actions, and beliefs, you can consciously work with your chakras in ways that increase your personal power, heal you, inspire you, and help you feel at home in the world. Chakra wisdom is a tool that will serve you throughout your lifetime, as both a vehicle of self-care and an amplifier of self-love.

What Is a Chakra?

The word *chakra* is most correctly pronounced CHALK-ruh, but more commonly pronounced SHOCK-ruh. (Take your pick.) In the ancient language of Sanskrit, *chakra* translates to "wheel." And it's not inaccurate to imagine your chakras like wheels of invisible light that emanate at certain areas along your spine. A term that can be used interchangeably with *chakra* is "energy center."

Before I orient you to each chakra, I want to point out some of the ways you've already experienced your chakras, perhaps without knowing it.

You've experienced your heart chakra opening when you looked at a kitten and felt like your heart might burst from all the cuteness. Or when a romantic partner looked at you in a certain way and you felt your heart "skip a beat."

You've experienced your third eye (the chakra at the center of your forehead) squeezing shut when you've been alerted to a problem that you weren't ready or willing to deal with and you suddenly developed a piercing headache.

You've experienced your throat chakra constricting when you were nervous to speak but you did it anyway and your voice came out in a shaky or strangled way.

You know when the magic and beauty of everything suddenly dawns on you and tears start streaming down your face? Maybe this has happened to you when you were with a loved one who was about to cross over to the other side, or when your grandchild was born, or when you were at a rave in the desert. Whatever the situation, when you have this experience, it means your crown chakra has opened.

You might say your chakra system is the energetic mechanics of your energy field, which is the intersection of your body, mind, and emotions. As you can see from the examples above, in much the same way that you can drive a car without understanding its mechanical dynamics, your chakra system works whether or not you are aware of its wiring, or even whether or not you are aware of it at all. But when you *are* aware of it, and aware of how you can consciously work with it in order to heal and nurture yourself as needed, you'll no longer get metaphorically stranded by the side of the road, waiting for enough reception to call a tow truck. You won't have to throw up your hands and say, "I don't know what's wrong! And I don't know how to fix it!" You can say, "Oh, I have a pounding headache. I think my third eye is closed up. First, let me take an aspirin (or Aleve or whatever you take), make sure I'm hydrated, and relax as best I can. Okay, now that the pain's starting to dissipate: what am I not wanting to look at, and how can I compassionately listen to the guidance that's trying to come through?" Or, "Oh, my heart's still hurting after the breakup. Let me breathe into that pain, feel compassion for myself, and send myself extra love. Let me remember the people and animals who love me who are still in my life, and feel gratitude for them."

Cultivating an awareness of your chakra system's dynamics helps you keep your personal energy field (remember: that's the intersection of your mind, body, and emotions) in good working order, so you're firing on all cylinders and you're regularly happy, healthy, radiant, powerful, balanced, and strong. Last but not least, being in tune with your chakra system unlocks endless tools for sending love to yourself regularly, and for consistently taking care of yourself on all the levels you are.

So let's take a look at the inner workings of your energy field, one chakra at a time.

Action Steps
• DISCOVER YOUR CHAKRAS •

As you read about your chakras, keep your journal or notebook handy and sit with your spine relatively straight in a comfortable way. This posture will allow energy to flow through your chakra system in the healthiest and most buoyant way, so that it will be easier to tune into each chakra as you read about it. You can sit on a meditation cushion on the floor, or you may want to sit up straight in a chair or sit cross-legged on a couch in a way that supports your back. Relax your shoulders away from your ears and take a few deep, conscious breaths. As you breathe in, imagine breathing energy down the front of your body to your tailbone. As you breathe out, imagine breathing energy up your spine from your tailbone to the crown of your head. Then let your breath be natural and relaxed.

Each chakra can help you love and care for yourself in its own special way.

Your root chakra is located at the tailbone area. If you're sitting as instructed above, you'll feel its placement more specifically by noticing where gravity is anchoring your body into your seat.

By making sure your root chakra is healthy, activated, and balanced, you support yourself in feeling connected to the earth, safe in your community and culture, and at home in your body and world. A healthy root chakra also helps you feel nourished by the physical world in the form of wealth, resources, comfortable shelter, and food.

Your root chakra spins horizontally, like a fan pointing directly down toward the floor. Even though most people don't see chakras with their physical eyes, the root chakra resonates at the same frequency as the color red.

Take a deep breath, and imagine that you're breathing energy all the way down into your ruby-red root chakra. As you breathe out, imagine your root chakra spinning more quickly and flinging off any stuckness, heaviness, or energetic debris. Breathe into it again and as you breathe out, inwardly see or sense it becoming brighter, healthier, more vibrant, and more balanced. Breathe all the way down to your root chakra one more time, and once more see it become more vibrant as you breathe out.

Next, place your palms flat on the chair, couch, or floor to either side of you. (This will help you connect your energy to the energy of the earth, which will amplify the primary dynamic of the root chakra.) Say or think the following statements while continuing to focus on and feel your root chakra area. Repeat each statement until it resonates emotionally with you as truth. If fears, worries, or negative thoughts come up while you do this, say hello to them. Smile at them. Feel them fully, breathe into them, ask yourself what it would feel like to let them go. And then, just for this moment, let them go. Imagine them dissipating and floating away right along with your exhale. Then, when you feel ready, come back to the statement. Take as long as you need with this:

I am safe.
Everything I need, I already have.
Mother Earth is my home.
I am at home in my body.
I am at home in my community.
I am at home in my world.

Now, in your notebook, jot down any messages or guidance you receive. You may see images or hear words in your mind, or you may have an inexplicable inner knowing or flash of understanding related to balancing and healing your root chakra and consequently feeling safe and at home in the world. For example, you may receive guidance about eating more substantial meals or eating more regularly throughout the day, releasing criticism about your body, taking daily walks in nature, or putting yourself in situations where you're apt to meet like-minded people so you can expand your community of supportive friends.

Your sacral chakra is located in your lower belly area, just below your navel. If you have a uterus (or even if you used to have a uterus or never had one and identify as female), the sacral chakra corresponds with the fertile energetic presence of your womb area. The intuition of all genders is intensely connected to this lower belly area, which is (along with the next chakra we'll talk about) what we often tune into when we say we have a "gut feeling" or "hunch." Place your hand on your lower belly area and take some deep breaths to connect with the deep inner wisdom that's always present within you.

The sacral chakra is deeply connected to your sense of self-love and body acceptance, as well as your sexual identity and your confidence in setting boundaries around who is allowed to touch your body or be present in your physical space and in what ways. This chakra is also aligned with choosing what physical locations and situations feel safe and nourishing to you. In other words, this area will alert you when you're not speaking your truth about your sexuality, when someone is violating your space, or when you're allowing yourself to stay somewhere that doesn't feel safe to you. The alerts often appear in the form of cramping, digestive issues, or tension that originates or manifests in the lower belly area.

If you've experienced any sort of physical or emotional abuse in the past, or if you've learned to disparage your sexuality or gender in any way, pain, discomfort, or medical issues may manifest in this area of your body until your stored trauma is healed and you restore your sense of personal sovereignty. For example, until I did some healing work on my sexual trauma and sexuality in general, I constantly seemed to be getting bladder infections. (Stress still manifests as pain or tension in this area for me sometimes, but it's not as systemic as it once was.)

Your sacral chakra spins vertically, like a pinwheel of radiant orange light just below your belly button. (This is the first of five vertically spinning chakras we'll discuss, and you can imagine all five of the vertically spinning chakras radiating and receiving energy in both the front and back of your body. For example, in this case, you can imagine the pinwheel of orange light emanating from both your lower belly and directly across from that area along your lower back. Still, most of us are more sensitized to the chakras in their location in the front of our bodies rather than the back. Some say the back emanation of chakras is more about your subconscious and stored emotions from the past, while the front emanation is more about your day-to-day consciousness and present-moment emotions. (For our purposes in this chapter, you can feel free to focus on feeling the five vertically spinning chakras in the front of your body.)

Place both hands on your lower belly and take a deep breath. Imagine you're breathing golden-white light straight into your lower belly area, nourishing and cleansing the vibrant orange wheel of light that is your sacral chakra. As you breathe out, imagine your sacral chakra spinning more quickly, and spinning off any stuck, dark, or heavy energy that may have been located in this area. Breathe light into this area a second time. Breathe out, and inwardly see the chakra spin more quickly and become even clearer, brighter, and more vibrant. Repeat with one more deep inhalation and exhalation.

Leave your hands on your lower belly and let your breath be natural while you continue to send breath and energy down to this chakra. Silently or aloud, speak the following statements as you do this. Continue repeating each one until it feels like you absolutely mean it and resonate with it. If you notice any negative thoughts or emotions coming up while you do this, allow them to be there. Smile to them, send breath to them, ask yourself what it would feel like to release them, and be willing to let them naturally dissolve in the light of your presence and awareness. Continue with one statement until your work with it feels complete, and then move on to the next:

My body is a safe harbor for me.
It is safe to be true to myself.
I tune into the way my body feels
before I make decisions.
I honor my personal space and honor
my intuition about my personal space.
I listen to what my body tells me about who
and what to allow in my personal space.
I fully and luxuriously inhabit my physical body.
I am in harmony with my unique sexuality.
I easily and naturally express my sexuality
in ways that feel safe to me.
I am naturally creative.
I gracefully flow with the changes of life.
I love birthing new ideas and conditions into the world.

Now clear your mind and connect your mind with your body by placing your attention on your breathing once again. When your mind feels centered and calm, see if you receive any messages about how to balance, heal, and harmonize your sacral chakra. You may see pictures in your mind's eye, hear or sense words or sentences, or a deep inner knowing may simply arise. In this case, the guidance may be related to sexuality, healthy boundaries, approving of your body, adorning and caring for your body, and feeling empowered to be, unapologetically, your unique and creatively expressive self. You may also receive more specific guidance, such as hobbies you want to try, articles of clothing you'd like to wear, or people you do or don't want to allow in your space. Whatever you do, don't judge the guidance you receive: trust it and know that it's relevant. Write it down in your journal. Be sure not to overthink this: just allow your consciousness to be fluid and open, and allow the guidance to flow out of your consciousness and onto the page.

Your solar plexus chakra is located above your navel and below your ribcage. When you feel empowered in your life, or in any situation, this area feels relaxed and open, and possibly even radiates a feeling of joy and well-being. When you feel disempowered, or in any way uncomfortable with the power that you hold, the area feels tense and unsettled, as if it is a radio attuned to a frequency of anxiety and unease. Place your hand there now and take a deep breath. When you do this, you're likely to tune right in to your current relationship with your personal power.

Your solar plexus chakra spins vertically, and vibrates at the same frequency as the color yellow. Imagine the bright, golden yellow vision of the sun. Now imagine it as a spinning circle about the diameter of an orange located above your belly button and below your rib cage. That's what your solar plexus chakra "looks" like.

If you regularly feel tension or discomfort in this area, you're not alone. I hear this complaint often, and have even experienced it myself in the past. For me, it finally cleared when I began writing regularly. Sitting down in front of my computer and letting my fingers type the words that wanted to flow through me finally released the stuck energy that had been uncomfortably building up in that area. Now I understand that writing is a fundamental expression of my personal power. So when I wasn't writing, I was suppressing a large portion of my power. It had nowhere to go, so it manifested as physical discomfort at my solar plexus area. Before I began the simple and straightforward process of writing on a regular basis, my sacral chakra had become like a toxic, festering pond. Writing transformed it into more of a fresh mountain stream.

Is there something you wish you could do and imagine it would feel powerful to do, but you tell yourself you wouldn't be good at it, or it would be too hard, or you have too much else to do anyway? If so, set aside at least thirty minutes, five times a week to do it (if it's a discipline like blogging or cooking), or to take steps toward it (if it's a goal like opening a business or getting a degree). It doesn't matter if you do it well. It doesn't mater if you take a giant step or a tiny one. It doesn't matter if you share what you did with anyone (for now). It just matters that you do it. Over time, the details will iron themselves out. But right away, you will likely discover a sense of comfortable lightness residing at your solar plexus area, which will become stronger and more pleasant the more regularly you allow your power to be expressed in this way.

Other reasons your solar plexus area may feel prickly, unsettled, or tense may include:

- Trusting outside concepts and standards over your own. For example, a) telling yourself you want to be a doctor because you know it will make your parents proud even though you really want to be a scuba instructor, or b) poring over fashion blogs to know what to wear this season rather than wearing what you like just because you like it.

- Doing things out of guilt or obligation and consequently ignoring your inner cries for more time to do the things *you* want to do.

- Believing you have to do, say, or act in ways that aren't authentic to you in order to please or placate others.

- Looking exclusively to others for your sense of validation and support.

- Believing any one person or group has the power to make you or break you.

- Believing you're stuck in any situation or condition.

- Believing that you don't have the power to choose what you do or how you experience life.

- In any way or on any level, giving away your power and/ or not realizing that you have the power to create positive change in your own life according to what you desire.

Place both hands on your solar plexus area and take a deep breath. Imagine you're breathing golden-white light into the center of your solar plexus. As you breathe out, inwardly see or sense your solar plexus chakra spinning more quickly and spinning off any stuck or heavy energy. Breathe light into your solar plexus. Breathe out and see it becoming even brighter, clearer, and more energized. Repeat with one more breath. Now let your breath be natural, but keep your attention on it: notice when you breathe in and notice when you breathe out. Stay with this until you feel balanced, centered, and calm.

Silently or aloud, repeat each of the following statements until it resonates with you on a deep level as truth. Then move on to the next. If any fears, worries, or limiting beliefs appear while you are working with these statements, smile to them and welcome them in. Feel the feelings associated with them, get curious about what it would feel like to let go of them, and on each exhale, be willing to breathe them out and let them go. Then, when you feel ready, come back to the statement:

I am one with the Infinite Power of the Universe.

I express my Infinite Power with confidence and joy.

If a relationship or situation doesn't resonate with me,

I am free to change it or let it go.

I am the sovereign authority in my own life.

No person, place, or thing has any power over me.

I am free to be who I am and do what I want.

I am free to express my personal
power in ways that bring me joy.

I prioritize myself. I prioritize my preferences.

I prioritize my desires.

I am aligned with my Infinite Self, so I always know
what I need to know, exactly when I need to know it.

I take inspired action calmly,
confidently, and with certainty.

Now, with your hands still on your solar plexus, breathe consciously once again. Take gentle note of your inhales and exhales until you feel centered and serene. Then open up your awareness to any messages you may receive about how to be in the world with relation to your solar plexus chakra. How can you be even more empowered? How can you take care of yourself fully by honoring your personal needs, opinions, and desires? How can you allow yourself to shine? What actions can you take, or new perspectives can you adopt? Again, allow this wisdom to come to you in any way: as words, thoughts, feelings, pictures, or a deep inner knowing or sensing. Whatever guidance you receive, write it down.

Your heart chakra is located at the center of your sternum or chest area. This is your emotional center. You know exactly where it is because it's the area that feels achy, warm, tender, or expansive when you feel love, empathy, longing, or grief. Living with an open heart chakra opens you up to emotional pain and vulnerability. So you might find yourself crying often or feeling intense sympathy with other beings who seem to be suffering. Despite the potential for pain, opening your heart chakra is more than worth it, because an open heart chakra is also what allows you to feel connected, inspired, and alive. When your heart chakra is open, you are indeed (to paraphrase poet Mary Oliver) making the very most of your one wild and precious life.[19]

Your heart chakra spins vertically, and resonates at the frequency of a vibrant emerald or aventurine green. In Sanskrit, the word for heart chakra is *anahata*, which can be translated to "un-struck." Some say this is because when our heart is open, we are bravely showing up in the world as if we've never been heartbroken or hurt. Others say that the heart center is filled with an alive, silent presence—a timeless openness—much like an unstruck gong, drum, or chime, possessing an eternity of silent potential, the pure formlessness that connects and underlies all things, beyond time and in all directions of time. I believe both metaphors are appropriate.

While the modern world is constantly providing messages, stories, situations, and potential situations that may cause us to want to close off our hearts, our ancestors in the ancient world

---

19. Mary Oliver, *House of Light: Poems by Mary Oliver* (Boston: Beacon Press, 2012).

were just as susceptible to wanting to insulate their hearts from pain. We are a species who loves deeply and who wants to be loved deeply. That alone opens us up to the not-unjustified fears of rejection, tragedy, and loss. Indeed, none of us emerge from this life unscathed by such painful experiences. We naturally react to this by wanting to shield and protect our hearts from trauma and anguish. The only problem with this is that it also shuts us off from fully feeling our love, which is the single most inspiring thing about being alive. It's what makes us feel connected and inspired. Without love, our lives have no meaning. If only we could shutter the windows of our hearts from the bitter winds of pain while still letting in all the sunshine of love! But we can't. It doesn't work that way. In this life experience, grief and love are so interconnected, when you examine them closely, you quickly realize they are one and the same.

We feel grief *because* we love. What is grief but an expression of how deeply we love? While we are all eternal at our core, within this experience of time and limitation, it is inevitable that we will witness the dissolution of the forms of people and animals and situations we love. This causes us to grieve.

By the same token, grief opens us up to love. When I consider the cats I have loved who are now on the other side, not only does my heart open to their precious feline spirits on the other side of the veil, my heart also opens to my cat Solo, who is still alive and present in this world. I'm reminded to treasure every precious, magical moment I have with him while he's still in this physical form. The same goes for my partner, Ted. When I hug him or walk down the street with him or binge-watch some new HBO show with him, I feel my love for him so much more completely when I remember that he will certainly die one day. And that I will certainly die one day. And if I'm being unflinchingly honest, that day could be tomorrow.

You might think considering your impending death or the impending death of someone you love is a downer. The truth is, *not* considering death is denial. And that denial doesn't only deny the truth of death, it denies the truth of life: its magic, preciousness, and depth. Living that way is a life half-lived. Which is why it's so crucial that we attend to our heart chakras, and keep them open as often and as fully as we can. Luckily, when you keep your heart chakra open, you can help soothe the pain associated with living in this world by sending *yourself* compassion and love. And that's exactly what you're about to do.

Place both hands (one on top of the other) on your heart chakra: the emotional center in the middle of your chest area. Take a deep breath, and see/imagine/sense that you're breathing golden-white light into the center of your heart chakra. As you exhale, imagine your heart chakra spinning more quickly. See it fling off and disperse any dark, heavy, or stuck energy and become an even brighter and more vibrant emerald color. Breathe in deeply once more and see your heart chakra filled with cleansing light. Breathe out and see it spin more quickly and become even clearer and more vibrant. Repeat this breathing pattern and visualization one more time.

With your hands still on your heart chakra, silently or aloud, say each of the following statements. Stay with each one until it resonates deeply for you as truth. Remember that if any negative feelings or limiting beliefs come up while you're working with these statements, completely welcome them in. Breathe in, feel the feelings associated with them. Then breathe out and be willing to let them go. If this feels tricky, you can always ask, "What would it feel like to let go of this challenging belief or feeling?"

Imagine the hypothetical freedom and breathe into it. Then see if you can let the feeling or belief go. Continue working with this releasing process until you feel clear and centered, and then come back to the statement. Take as long as you need:

I fully open my heart to love.
I know that I am lovable.
I am a beloved child of the Universe, and I am lovable.
I am loved.
I open my heart and allow myself to love.
Love is infinite, so there is enough love for everyone, including me.
I am courageous. I open my heart to all my feelings.
I feel my feelings so I can heal my feelings.
I bravely open my heart to love.
I generously give love.
I fully receive love.
I love and treasure myself.
I love you, [your name here].
I am love.

Begin once again to breathe consciously: notice when you inhale and notice when you exhale, and breathe light and healing into your heart area. Open up your consciousness to any guidance you may receive regarding your heart chakra. Again, be open to receiving this guidance in any way: through mental pictures or words, emotions or physical sensations, or just a deep inner knowing. These messages may obviously relate to the heart chakra and emotions, or the connection may not be immediately obvious. Whatever intuitions or words of wisdom you receive, note them in your journal.

Your throat chakra emanates from and encompasses your entire neck and throat area. It spins vertically and is aligned with the clean, clear blue of the sky once the clouds clear and the sun reemerges after a rainstorm.

If you like to sing (for an audience or just by yourself), you know the joy that comes along with a healthy and activated throat chakra. Chanting during meditation or yoga has a similarly soothing and activating effect on this energy center. And whatever your relationship may be with public speaking at this point in time, you can bet it resonates at your throat chakra. If you love it, your throat chakra hums at a healthy vibration while you do it. If you loathe it, your throat chakra constricts at the very thought of it.

What's more, how you respond to your feelings about public speaking (or speaking your truth in general) always has an effect on your throat chakra. For example, let's say you're about to make a toast at your sister's wedding. You walk up to the front of the room not only with butterflies in your stomach, but also with a feeling of tension in your neck and constriction in your throat. But when you override that feeling and begin speaking anyway, the constriction begins to clear. You start to relax and enjoy communicating in this way. As you do so, the energy center at your throat opens up like a rose and begins to spin more quickly and shine more brightly. The same goes for when you are afraid to speak up about something but you finally push through the fear and do it anyway.

On the other hand, some people have an energetic imbalance at the throat chakra the results in too *much* talking. We've all run into nervous talkers who hate dead air so much that they have to fill every silence by saying something, whether or not they actually have something to say. We've also all encountered people who are so enthusiastic about sharing their thoughts that they don't seem to let anyone else get a word in edgewise. And if we're being honest, many of us can probably think of times that *we* were those people. (I know I can.)

In short, a healthy and balanced throat chakra corresponds with a healthy and balanced relationship with communication. This means being comfortable with saying what's true for you, and it also means not speaking when you have nothing to say. It means putting your two cents in as you feel guided while also being interested in what others have to say, allowing them time to speak, and listening deeply to both their words and the unspoken meaning behind the words. Some days this will mean that you do a lot of talking, while other days it will mean that you do a lot of listening. Most days will be a bit of both.

Self-expression in general corresponds with the throat chakra: it isn't limited to audible communication. It includes artistic expression, communicating through the written word, and expressing yourself through your actions, expressions, or style choices. If it's a form of communication, it resides in the realm of the throat chakra.

Gently place the fingertips of both hands on each side of your throat in a way that feels comfortable and loving. Breathe in and imagine golden-white light filling your throat chakra. Breathe out and see/imagine/sense this sky-blue chakra spinning more quickly and spinning off any dark, stuck, or heavy energy or any energetic debris. Breathe light into the center of this chakra. Breathe out and see it becoming brighter and more vibrant as it spins more rapidly. Repeat this cleansing breath one more time.

With your fingers still gently resting on each side of your throat, silently or aloud speak the following affirmative statements. Stay with each following statement until it resonates with you as truth. Welcome any limiting thoughts or challenging feelings that come up. Allow them in fully as you breathe in. As you exhale, be open to letting them go. The more you do this, the closer you will be to accepting the statement as true for you:

It is easy and natural for me to speak my truth.
I express myself fully and effortlessly.
I love expressing my unique perspectives and beliefs.
I honor the unique perspectives and beliefs of others.
I spend time with people who listen to me
and want to hear what I have to say.
When other people talk, I get quiet and listen.
I feel comfortable expressing what is true for me.
Even if it's temporarily uncomfortable or awkward,
I say what I need to say.
I say what I need to say because I respect myself.
I love expressing myself creatively.
I express myself freely and in wonderful ways.
I honor my voice and allow it to be heard.
I honor the voices of others and allow them to be heard.

I express what I need to express, even if what I have to say may not be what someone wants to hear.
I speak my truth with love.

Return your awareness to your breath: notice as you breathe in and notice as you breathe out. Be sensitive to any messages you may receive about your throat chakra, such as behaviors or perspectives you might adopt or change in order to support the health of this energy center. Just as with the previous chakras, you may receive these messages in any number of ways. Whatever you receive, trust it. And write it down in your journal.

Your third eye chakra is located at your forehead, about an inch or so above the center of your eyebrows. When you say to yourself, "Time to focus," or, "Let me think," or, "Let's see, I'll bet I can figure this out," you crease your brow and move your awareness to this energy center. That's because it has to do with seeing deeply into the nature of things and using your thought and visioning power to bring about the outcome you desire. It also has to do with seeing on many levels: your physical eyes, after all, do a great job of seeing the physical world. The third eye is where you see *beyond* the physical, by seeing how invisible factors (such as emotions, beliefs, ideas, possibilities, and subtle energies) influence conditions in the past, present, or future.

The third eye is just as powerful as the other chakras, but it seems to be somewhat more compact, which makes it more energetically concentrated. It spins vertically and resonates at the vibration of a deep, indigo blue.

In some cases, challenges with the third eye chakra can cause headaches. For example, I recently read a book called *Chaos: Charles Manson, the CIA, and the Secret History of the Sixties*. And I loved it! I don't regret reading it one bit. But it did overburden my third eye chakra at one point. It's too long and complex a book to paraphrase here, but let's just say it was written by a journalist who spent twenty years going down a terrifying rabbit hole. When I was maybe about halfway through, I was thinking about so many possibilities and connecting so many dots that my third eye became overwhelmed and a pounding headache ensued. To this day, when I try to have a conversation about the things I read in this book, I can feel a headache coming on.

I wouldn't go so far as to say that third eye overload is *always* the catalyst for headaches. But I would say that it's always tied in there somehow. I mean, if you go a day without your usual cup of coffee, the blood vessels in your brain constrict and give you a headache. But caffeine also has an effect on your third eye chakra, as does going without it when you're used to it. (In this case, and in the case of chakras in general, pain or health challenges that manifest in the general vicinity of any given chakra are not always *caused* by the chakra, but the two factors *are* often correlated. So if a health challenge lies at or near a chakra point, attending to that chakra will likely provide insight and an opportunity for healing.)

When your third eye is relaxed and open, you're insightful, focused, and intuitive. You see into the heart of things and naturally bolster your understanding of people, situations, and events with an unspoken awareness of their subtle and energetic underpinnings. You won't know *everything*, but you'll have access to whatever insight will most benefit you in the moment.

Close your eyes and lightly rest the pad of your dominant index finger (right if you're right-handed, left if you're left-handed) on your third eye: the center of your forehead just above your eyebrows. Take a deep breath in and imagine you're breathing golden white light into the center of this chakra. Breathe out and see or sense this compact wheel of indigo light spinning faster and flinging off any stuck or congested energy. Take another deep breath in and breathe light into the center of your third eye. Breathe out and see your third eye becoming brighter, clearer, and more vibrant. Repeat one more such cleansing breath. Then, silently or aloud and while keeping your finger on your third eye chakra, open your eyes and speak or think the following statements. Again, repeat one until it resonates for you as something you truly believe. When and if challenging thoughts, feelings, or beliefs arise, smile to them. Invite them in fully as you breathe in. And then gently release your hold on them as you breathe out. Stay with this until the negative emotional charge is no longer present:

I see clearly.
I perceive deeply.
I know that I don't need to know everything,
and find it easy to admit when I don't know.
When I do know, I trust that knowing.
I know what I need to know when I need to know it.
I trust my intuition.
I pay attention to my intuition,
even when I don't logically understand it.

I have the ability to see into the heart of things.
I open my eyes to the beauty that surrounds me.
I allow myself to perceive the perfection
that transcends and underlies All That Is.
When I see other people through eyes of love, they heal.
When I see the world through
eyes of love, the world evolves.
When I see myself through eyes of love, I flourish.

Once again, focus on your breathing. Notice as you breathe in and out. With your finger still on your third eye, open up to any messages you may receive about keeping your third eye chakra vibrant and healthy. Don't discount any messages you receive simply because you can't see a logical connection. Trust what you sense, feel, know, or see with your inner awareness. And make a note of every bit of guidance that comes through.

Your crown chakra is located at the top of your head, where a small beanie would be placed if you were wearing one on the very highest point of your scalp. Imagine your crown chakra as a ceiling fan of diamond-white and vibrant violet light, spinning horizontally.

The crown chakra is where we feel connected to everything: open to Infinity. As I mentioned earlier in this chapter, it's a sure sign your crown chakra is open if you find yourself crying because life is so spectacularly and incomprehensibly beautiful.

There's a Chinese fable about a frog who lived in a well. I'm not exactly sure where I read it, but I'm pretty sure I read it in a book on Buddhism when I was a senior in high school. This is probably not how it is written, but this is how I remember it:

Once upon a time, there was a frog who lived in a well. One day, a turtle looked down into the well and said, "Wow, this is a nice place you have here."

The frog responded, "Oh hey, thanks. Have you got one of these too?"

The turtle said, "Well, no. Actually I live in the sea."

"The sea? What's that?"

"It's a lot of water in one place. Much, much more water than you have here in this well."

The frog thought for a moment. "So, you're saying your ocean is, like, twice as big as my well?"

The turtle smiled and said, "Oh no, no! It's much bigger than that."

The frog felt this strained his new friend's credibility, but he politely responded, "Hmm. Okay. Three times as big?"

The turtle laughed and said, "Let me show you. Come with me."

So the frog hopped along behind the turtle, who led them both toward his home by the sea. When they came upon the vast expanse of water and rolling waves, the frog took one look... And then his head exploded.

(The end.)

Most of the time in modern life, we are the frog living in his little world, completely unaware of the sea. But sometimes, when we brush against Infinity and transcend the limited view of our personal stories, our heads explode. In other words: our crown chakras open. Sometimes this is rapturous and other times it's harrowing.

The metaphor of the exploding head is similar to what we mean when we say something is "mind-blowing." This may also be described as a (usually temporary) obliteration of the ego. (If you remember, the ego may be defined as the illusion of separation, or in other words our limited view of ourselves and our place in the Universe.) In Buddhism, when the obliteration of the ego is not temporary but permanent—permanent "head explosion" and ego eradication—it's called *nirvana,* which is a term our culture has not inaccurately associated with terms such as heaven, ecstasy, and bliss. (And also the grunge music scene of the 1990s, but that's a whole other thing.)

Whenever you're able to do so, go outside in nature (or even your backyard) and find a comfortable place to sit where you won't be distracted or disturbed. Sit comfortably, with your spine relatively straight in a natural way. Sit on the earth if you can, but if it's more comfortable for you, sitting in a chair will work just as well. Feel gravity anchoring you in the physical plane. Begin to breathe consciously: notice when you breathe in and notice when you breathe out. Become aware of your root chakra: the place where gravity is holding you onto the earth. Take a deep breath and breathe light and energy into your root chakra. Breathe out and sense your root chakra becoming clearer and brighter. Repeat this single cleansing breath process with your sacral chakra (at your lower belly area), your solar plexus chakra (at your upper belly area), your heart chakra (at the center of your sternum), your throat chakra (at your neck area), and your third eye chakra (in the center of your forehead).

Now, breathe into your crown chakra at the very top of your scalp. Breathe light into it. As you breathe out, inwardly sense it spinning more quickly and spinning off any darkness, heaviness, or debris. Breathe light into it a second time, and on this breath, as you breathe out, become aware of the vast expanse of the sky. Invite that vastness into your crown chakra. One more time: breathe light into your crown chakra. Breathe out and feel this vibrant, blindingly bright wheel of light opening up like a flower and inviting in an awareness of Infinity, and of your own infinite nature.

Now, silently or aloud, repeat the following statements. Stay with each one until it resonates for you as truth. If limiting beliefs or challenging feelings arise, smile to them, welcome them in, and then, just as easily, let them go:

I open my awareness to Infinity.
I expand my sense of self to include Infinity.
I am Infinity.
I am Infinite Love.
I am Infinite Peace.
I am Infinite Wisdom.
I know my true identity as a child of Infinity.
I am pure wisdom, pure empowerment, pure truth.
I am one with All That Is.
I am eternal: beyond birth and death,
beyond time and space.
The truth of who I am is Divine.

Return your awareness to your breath. Place your palms flat on the earth (or chair) next to you to physically connect to the physical plane. As you breathe consciously, remember that you can be aware of your Infinity while also being fully present and attentive within this physical existence. You can be the frog *and* the turtle. You can easily move between the two realities and perspectives with ease.

. . . .

I hope you've enjoyed this journey through the rainbow of your being. It's a journey that will continue throughout your lifetime, helping you detect and clear energetic and emotional blockages, and opening you up more and more to your own beauty and magic, as well as the empowerment that comes from knowing that you are a glorious refraction of the One Light that gives birth to all that we see.

Thirteen
REMEDIES AND RITUALS FOR THE SPIRALING PATH

Your path through the enchanted forest of life will not be a straight one. It will spiral and swirl, and you'll find yourself returning again and again to many of the same challenges and issues, even if the form they take has changed. Remember way back in the very first chapter when I said learning to love yourself isn't like learning to ride a bike? It's true. It's more like an entire lifetime of avid chess playing: knowing—and even hoping—all the while that there will always be an opponent (i.e., a situation, condition, or relationship) that can challenge you, teach you something in a new way, and ultimately steer you closer to the center of your mastery.

I recently posted this meme on my social media pages, along with the image of a spiral: "Spiritual Path Definition: Learning the same things, over and over again." Some people responded with crying or pouting faces, or with stories of their current heartache or woe. Others seemed to interpret it the way I did: as not only truthful, but also liberating. The fact is, if you're still here, you're still learning. You can lament that fact or you can celebrate it. I choose to celebrate. An adventure is not an adventure without a challenge. A static point of perfection is *not* perfection: it's stagnation.

I want to drive this point home because for years this was something I didn't understand, and my not understanding it caused me a lot of suffering. I would seem to reach a certain level of self-approval or free myself from a certain emotional dark cloud, and I would be ecstatic, skipping around and praising the beauty of everything. Then I would wake up one day and feel down on myself again and believe that I had failed. Or maybe I would snap at someone or get drunk and say something embarrassing or do something else I didn't approve of and berate myself for it. "I'm never going to get this spiritual evolution thing right," I would think, "because here I am again, back at square one. Back in the dumps."

Eventually, I realized that it *wasn't* square one, and it didn't have to be the dumps. It was another loop on the spiral. The idea of linear evolution was just an idea I had picked up in elementary school: you learn addition, then subtraction, then multiplication, then division. You learn to recite the alphabet, and then write the alphabet, and then you learn to read. When I realized this model doesn't remotely apply to personal development, I felt so free. It turned out the worst part of coming up against a particular challenge was usually not the challenge itself, but rather the degree to which I beat myself up about it. Trying to live up to an unattainable standard will make anyone depressed. And please understand: getting to a place where you have no more potential to learn *is* unattainable. And even if it *were* a real thing, can you imagine how boring it would be? Ugh.

It's a natural trick of the human mind to imagine that there *are* people out there who have reached an inviolable state of perfection. That's why we must be vigilant in reminding ourselves, again and again and again: *zero* human beings are perfect. *Every person on Earth* comes back around to similar challenges throughout their lifetimes (no matter how famous they are, how often they meditate, or how many seemingly flawless photos they post on social media). So we might as well do our best to bring lightness to this process. We might as well laugh, be kind to ourselves, and enjoy the messy, bumpy, perfectly imperfect ride.

When you surrender to the process of constant learning and growth, you stop feeling stuck. You realize that every incarnation of a certain problem is like a new level of a video game: similar, but also different. Perhaps it's more colorful, fast-paced, or exciting. You might say that each new version of any given challenge will open you up to a greater level of enlightenment, while simultaneously allowing you to enjoy the level of enlightenment you've already attained.

All that being said, think of this chapter as a resource and roadmap you can come back to again and again throughout your spiraling journey. If you're running into a certain challenge, look for a ritual or remedy that corresponds. Approach it in the spirit of enjoying the playful process of your evolution while supporting your advancement to the next level of the game. And if none of these rituals or remedies are quite what you're looking for, adapt one of them, combine more than one of them, or create one of your own. When you perform a ritual or healing practice like the ones in this chapter, the single most important thing is that you know precisely why you're doing it: that you approach it with a clear and defined intent. That's where the power lies: not in doing the ritual or enlisting the remedy, but in the intention you put behind it. Think of any action you take as a way of clearly demonstrating your intention to yourself and the Universe, which is a way of helping to set your intention in motion.

To illustrate the dynamics of a ritual, consider a couple of popular mainstream ritual scenarios: weddings and graduations. Do you have to get married publicly in order to make a lifelong commitment to someone? Do you have to wear one of those weird hats in order to obtain a degree? No to both! But many people choose to participate in a ritual of commitment (i.e., a *wedding*) in order to demonstrate their feelings and intentions to themselves, their partner, and their loved ones. And many graduates participate in a ritual of initiation (i.e., a *graduation*) in order to symbolize to themselves and their families that they've reached a certain level of knowledge and expertise, and are ready to advance to another phase of their career. A ritual is a way of anchoring your intention in your psyche and broadcasting it to the Universe by taking a clear, decisive, symbolic action in the physical world.

Don't discount the power of the exercises in this chapter. As you've seen from the exercises in the previous chapters, bringing your full attention to a simple ritual or self-care practice can be a surprisingly effective way to bring about positive change. After all, what you send out energetically (with your thoughts, feelings, intentions, and actions) really does come back to you multiplied. But you don't have to take my word for it! Approach your ritual work with a spirit of experimentation and discover its effectiveness for yourself.

Remedy
• CLEAR OVERWHELM •

If you feel overwhelmed in general, or in any life area, it's time once more to clear your clutter. It sounds simple, but it always, *always* helps with overwhelm of any kind. If you have a lot of clutter that can be cleared, clear clutter from one limited area, like your medicine cabinet or your sock drawer. Then, repeat tomorrow or the next time you have a moment to clear. Digital clutter like old emails, photos, and downloads also counts. Continue until your feeling of overwhelm is transformed into clarity and calm. Cleaning and organizing can also help. And remember to take all this action with the clear intention to clear your mind and establish greater harmony and peace. Consider playing music or lighting a candle to make it into more of an event.

Ritual
• SPEAK YOUR TRUTH •

Is there something you need to say in order to stand up for what's right? Perhaps you've been treated in a way that seems unfair and you've tried to forget about it, but it just doesn't feel right not to speak up. But on the other hand, something is holding you back: perhaps you don't want to deal with the drama, or to be seen as a squeaky wheel, or maybe you fear that you'll be ridiculed or bullied if you go ahead and say what is true for you. If any of this resonates with what you're going through, try the following ritual.

Light a sky-blue candle on your altar, or somewhere else where you can sit quietly for a few minutes without being disturbed. Take three deep, conscious breaths and then allow your breath to become natural while remaining attentive to your breathing. Notice as you breathe in. Notice as you breathe out. Stay with this until your body feels relaxed and your mind feels centered. Now bring to mind the person or people with whom you feel called to speak. Allow any emotions to arise in relation to this person or group of people. Perhaps you feel anger, for example. If so, feel that anger fully. Breathe it in and allow it completely. As you breathe out, let the energy behind the feeling go with the breath. If you're not sure if you want to let it go, imagine what it would feel like if you *did* let it go. Then simply be *willing* to let it go. Repeat with the same emotion until it shifts or clears. Then see if another emotion arises, such as fear, or pain, or indignation. Feel it as you breathe in and release it as you breathe out. Again, stay with it for as long as it takes for it to clear or start to shift.

The point of this is to let go of any sense that you're a victim or any belief that this person or group has any sort of power over you. That way, when you speak your truth, it can come from a place of empowerment rather than from the illusion that you are vulnerable to the whim of someone else's opinion of you or behavior toward you. So by going through this breathing and releasing process, the idea is to get in touch with what you actually need to say instead of any disempowering stories you may have been telling yourself about the situation.

With this in mind, once any negative emotional charge seems to be significantly diminished, imagine sending a cord of energy from your root chakra down to the core of the earth. Breathe golden-white light up from the core of the earth, through your root chakra, and straight into your aura. Next, send a pillar of light up from your crown chakra out of the earth's atmosphere and into the diamond-white light of Infinity. Breathe this light down the pillar, into your crown chakra, and into your aura. Feel your entire body and the sphere of light around your body glowing and swirling with nourishing, protective light. Say, silently or aloud, "I am safe. I am safe to speak my truth. I let go of all fear of how others will react. I see the best in others, and I speak to them with love." Feel your throat area glowing and swirling with a healing, balancing, sky-blue light.

Feel gratitude to the earth. Feel gratitude to the cosmos. Then go forth and speak. Make the phone call, send the email, make the appointment, or physically approach the person or people to whom you need to speak. When you do so, send compassion to yourself. If you feel fear or reluctance at any point, place a your hand on your heart or belly, or discreetly give yourself a hug and remember that all humans have moments when they feel uncertain and afraid. Have compassion for yourself through the process. Return to what's true for you. And if you notice yourself getting defensive, take a deep breath and remember the light around you and within you. Remember you are safe.

Remedy
• LOVE YOUR BODY •

Has anyone grown up in this culture unscathed by body judgment and shame? It's hard to imagine so. With this in mind, it's important that you have patience with yourself if negative self-talk about your body happens to arise. For Goddess's sake, don't let the ideal of body positivity become one more excuse to beat yourself up.

Instead, let it be a portal into loving yourself more. Feel compassion for yourself, and even let a sense of fierce protectiveness be inspired within you when you feel the judgmental voice of body-negative culture arise within you. In the excellent book *The Body Is Not an Apology,* author Sonya Renee Taylor calls that critical, judgmental voice your "outside voice." It doesn't come from you. It comes from outside of you. When you notice your outside voice encroaching on your peace, shift to using what she calls your "inside voice," the voice within you that's your authentic self. That voice doesn't see any problem with your body's natural size, shape, and appearance. Weed out the voice you got stuck in your head like an annoying song, and listen to the voice that's always echoing from deep within your center, sending resounding messages of self-approval and self-love.

As a ritual of anchoring yourself in your "inside voice," obtain an aventurine stone. It can be just a polished stone or set in some sort of jewelry setting like a pendant, bracelet, or ring. Empower it in bright sunlight for two to five minutes. Then keep it with you as needed as a reminder to repeatedly and lovingly shift to speaking to and about yourself with your authentic inner voice of body positivity and love. When you come back to doing this again and again, eventually it will become a habit.

Ritual
• SET BOUNDARIES •

As we discussed in chapter 6, when any relationship challenge arises, setting positive boundaries will help you deal with it and heal it effectively. If you realize it's time to set some clearer boundaries, you might want to start with rereading that chapter to refresh your boundary IQ. Then, if you'd like a little extra support, you can perform the following ritual.

Create or obtain a necklace or pendant containing one or more mirrored tiles of any shape or size. Light a candle (on your self-love altar or somewhere else where you won't be disturbed) and sit comfortably in front of it with your spine straight in a relaxed way. Take some deep, conscious breaths to center your-self and align your mind, body, and spirit. Hold the mirrored necklace in both hands. Become aware of your grounding cord connecting you to the golden light at the center of the earth and the pillar of light at the top of your head connecting you with the infinite, diamond-white light of the cosmos. Feel these ener-gies merging and mixing within you, and especially pooling at your heart area. Then, send this powerful light from your heart, through your arms, into your hands, and finally feel it gathering and pulsating within the necklace.

Say, "Anything that is not of my energy is swiftly and com-pletely reflected back to its source. I am grounded in earth and sky. I am centered in myself. I am safe and all is well." Fasten the necklace around your neck.

Feel and sense a powerful sphere of light around you and feel safe within that light. Also sense and know that the mirrored charm will remind you to clearly discern where you end and oth-ers begin, and will additionally remind you to speak your truth and be true to yourself in all ways. Send gratitude to the earth. Send gratitude to the cosmos. Send gratitude to yourself. Smile and know that all is well.

Remedy
• CLEAR THE FEAR •

We all feel fear, to some degree, pretty much every single day: whether we call it anxiety, unease, worry, panic, terror, shyness, or distress. Sometimes we don't even name it: we just feel our heart rate speed up, our breath become short, or our brow begin to perspire. Or we just quietly avoid something.

If you're like most of us, you feel at least a little fear every time you get into a car, meet someone new, say goodbye to a loved one, or consider speaking up about something that's important to you. Fear is a natural part of being a mortal, social being on Earth. That's why our first order of business when it comes to dealing with fear is to give up the battle against it. We'll never defeat it: it will always come back. So we may as well be like the renowned spiritual teacher Thich Nhat Hanh, who, when fear arises within him, inwardly greets it with the words, "Fear, old friend, I recognize you." [20]

Indeed, saying "yes" or "hello" or "welcome" is the place to start when dealing with any uncomfortable emotion, including fear. Surrender is the only way to begin to stop the war within.

The next time fear arises within you and you notice it, you can loosen its hold on you and help clear it out of your body and mind by placing one hand on your belly and one hand on your heart. Close your eyes. Breathe in and think, "Breathing in, I say hello to my fear." Breathe out and think, "Breathing out, I let it be." Breathe in again and think, "Breathing in, I smile to my fear." Breathe out and think, "Breathing out, I let it go." (This pattern of breath and inner self-talk is inspired by, but not identical to, mindfulness meditations by Thich Nhat Hanh.) Stay with this for as long as it takes to turn the tide, and feel free to make the statements your own. The key is the energy and intention behind them, so it doesn't matter what words you use as long as you breathe in and welcome the feeling, and then breathe out and do your best to let go. All the while, be sure to send yourself plenty of compassion and love.

---

20. Thich Nhat Hanh, *Touching Peace: Practicing the Art of Mindful Living* (Berkeley, CA: Parallax Press, 2005), 29.

Remedy
• DISCOVER YOUR DESIRES •

Have you ever seen the movie *Clueless*? What the title actually refers to is how the main character, Cher (played by Alicia Silverstone), is so completely in the dark about what she wants (or rather *who* she wants) through almost the entire film. I know this has happened to me before, more than once. It's amazing how we're such complex psychological beings that we can actually conceal our desires from ourselves! So thoroughly! And then once we realize them, we can look back and see that all the obvious clues were there. We just, for whatever reason, couldn't (or wouldn't) allow ourselves to see them. The truth is, we usually know what we want, even when we don't know that we know.

If you're presently clueless about what you actually want in any given situation, whether it's related to whom you want to be with, what career you want to try, where you want to live, or anything else, try this: on a piece of paper, write, "I know what I want to do about [my love life, my career path, etc.]" Or, you could write, "I know where I want to live," "I know what I want to do," or even just, "I know exactly what I want." Slide this paper between your mattress and your box spring, with the words facing up. (If you just sleep on a mattress without a box spring, just slide it directly under the mattress, facing up.)

Then, literally, *sleep on it.* Don't rush a conclusion. Whether you ruminate on the issue excessively or put it out of your mind completely, it doesn't matter! Whenever you need to know, you'll know. And when that day comes, you can simply remove the paper from beneath your mattress and throw it in a recycling bin. (Or throw it on a fire it if you prefer to be dramatic like that.)

Ritual
• HEAL A RELATIONSHIP DYNAMIC •

Notice the name of this ritual is not "Heal a Relationship." It's "Heal a Relationship *Dynamic*." That's because if you're having a challenge in a relationship, chances are good that it's not unique to that relationship. Until the challenging dynamic *itself* is healed, it will keep showing up again and again in one form or another. And that's not because of the other person.

Okay, actually, it *is* about the other person in some ways, but not in any ways you can control. What you *can* control is whatever belief, habit, or expectation—within *you*—is causing you to attract and perpetuate this dynamic.

The challenge you're experiencing is likely born from a pattern you inadvertently picked up along the way in this lifetime or another, such as a lack of belief in your self-worth or a fear that you'll lose someone if you're honest with them about who you really are or what you really think. Whatever the pattern, it could even be something you inherited from your family: something that was set in motion centuries before you were even born. The point is that you are not to blame for this pattern, or the relationship dynamic it's holding in place. But if you want to heal the pattern, it *is* your responsibility. No one else is going to do it for you. (Although of course you can always seek out support in healing yourself, in the form of a therapist or a supportive friend. Indeed, if you have a deep and long-standing relationship challenge, working with a therapist would be an excellent idea.)

When you heal a relationship dynamic, it may look a number of ways. Some relationships will end. Others will fade away. Still others will improve. Regardless of the outward appearance, the outcome will be the same in this way: you'll be healed and whole. Your relationships, moving forward, will be healthier and more supportive than they were before. You'll begin to more easily attract partners and friends who are genuinely good for you. You'll feel more comfortable in your skin. Your joy will begin to emerge like the sun after a rainstorm. And you'll be free.

Open to the first blank page in your journal and write down every emotion you can think of related to the relationship dynamic you want to heal. How do you feel when you think about this challenge? How do you feel when you're in the middle of it? What feelings are underneath those feelings? What feelings are you afraid to admit or feel? Take your time be honest with yourself. Go deep.

Next, list times in the past that you've felt a similar way. How far back can you trace this relationship pattern? What's the earliest time you remember feeling this particular kind of pain?

Take a break from brainstorming and place one hand on your belly and one hand on your heart. Remind yourself that all humans suffer: we all feel emotional pain. We all have relationship challenges. Send yourself compassion for the challenges you've experienced in the past and the challenges you're experiencing now.

Now, lovingly look at the beliefs and expectations that are behind these feelings and this pattern. Is it possible this pattern comes from a belief that you have to defend yourself constantly in order to escape emotional pain? Or perhaps that you don't deserve to be treated with kindness? Or that you aren't worth listening to? Or that relationships are always hard?

Or maybe if you're honest, you can see that you've been so focused on your own experience that you haven't fully considered how much pain the other person may be in. Perhaps, through the lens of compassion, you can see why they may be hurting, or why they may be lashing out. Move through this investigation process with curiosity. Remember, this is not about judgment or finding reasons to blame yourself. You can look at the whole situation, and everyone involved, through eyes of love.

Finally, look at everything you've written and see how you can rewrite the challenge for yourself. Look especially at the limiting beliefs or expectations. For example, if you've written, "I believe I don't deserve love," you might rewrite that belief as, "I deserve love," or "I am worthy of love." If you've discovered that you haven't sufficiently explored the other person's perspective, you could rewrite that challenge as, "I listen deeply. I open my heart to the experience of others." And if you see a pattern from your past that hurt you in a way that caused you to continue to expect or manifest similar pain, you might write, "I have compassion for the pain I experienced in the past. And now I'm willing to let it go, so I can step into a beautiful new present and future."

Transfer your rewritten beliefs and patterns from your journal to a note card or individual piece of paper, or make a note of them on your phone. Then take a walk outside. As you walk, consider one positive statement at a time. Ruminate on it as you gaze at the flowers and the clouds, and listen to the birds singing, the sound of your feet, and the wind blowing through the trees. Repeat it to yourself and roll it over in your mind. Let it slowly begin to rewire your brain. Keep walking until you've taken at least a few minutes with each statement.

Before you go to sleep, read over your rewrites once more. In the morning, you'll very likely have some guidance about the next steps to take with regards to the present relationship challenge as well as your healing journey.

CONCLUSION

Self-love really is a superpower. It's a process of learning to welcome what arises within you, and also learning not to beat yourself up when you don't. I'll say it again: it's a spiral, not a line. It's a journey, not a destination. And now that you've made it to the end of the book, it's safe to say you're on that journey. And the whole spiraling journey is also all there within you, just as an acorn already possesses the entirety of the oak.

Just one more thing before you go: This superpower? It's contagious! The more you dare to love yourself, the more you inspire self-love in others. Nothing liberates or heals or empowers like love, and love starts with you. And after all you've experienced as you've made your way through this book, I'm certain you've caught at least a fleeting glimpse of how lovable you are, and how absolutely blindingly brilliant your soul really is. So go spread the self-love superpower like the sun spreads light throughout the sky. Go forth and live. Go forth and love. Go forth and shine.

RESOURCES

christyharrison.com

magicmondaypodcast.com

mollykatewellness.com

mothermeera.com

tesswhitehurst.com

BIBLIOGRAPHY

Boyd, C. et al. "Psychological Features Are Important Predictors of Functional Gastrointestinal Disorders in Patients with Eating Disorders." *Scandinavian Journal of Gastroenterology* 40, no. 8 (2005): 929–35.

Brown, Brené. *Daring Greatly: How the Courage to Be Vulnerable Transforms the Way We Live, Love, Parent and Lead.* New York: Penguin, 2013.

_____. *The Gifts of Imperfection: Let Go of Who You Think You're Supposed to Be and Embrace Who You Are.* Center City, MN: Hazelden, 2010.

Cameron, Julia. *The Artist's Way: A Spiritual Path to Higher Creativity.* New York: Tarcher, 1992.

Campbell, Joseph. *The Hero with a Thousand Faces.* New York: Pantheon Books, 1949.

"Codependency." *Merriam-Webster.* July 2020. https://www.merriam-webster.com/dictionary/codependency.

Domet, Stephanie. "Living Greatly." *Mindful,* December 2019: 52–63.

Dooner, Caroline. *The F*ck It Diet: Eating Should Be Easy.* New York: HarperCollins, 2019.

Dwoskin, Hale. *The Sedona Method: Your Key to Lasting Happiness, Success, Peace, and Emotional Well-being.* Sedona, AZ: Sedona Press, 2003.

Fagan, Abigail. "Immersed in Perfection." *Psychology Today.* February 2020: 28–30.

Greene, Robert. *The Laws of Human Nature.* New York: Viking, 2018.

Hafiz. *The Gift: Poems by Hafiz.* New York: Penguin Compass, 1999.

Hanh, Thich Nhat. *Touching Peace: Practicing the Art of Mindful Living.* Berkeley, CA: Parallax Press, 2005.

Harrison, Christy. *Anti-Diet: Reclaim Your Time, Money, Well-Being, and Happiness Through Intuitive Eating.* New York: Little, Brown Spark, 2019.

Hay, Louise L. *You Can Heal Your Life.* Carlsbad, CA: Hay House, 1984.

Judith, Anodea. *Chakras: Seven Keys to Awakening and Healing the Energy Body.* Carlsbad, CA: Hay House, 2016.

Leander, Richard. "The Invisible Kingdom." *Wonder-World: A Collection of Fairy Tales, Old and New.* London: George Bell and Sons, 1875.

Nagosaki, Emily. *Come As You Are: The Surprising New Science That Will Transform Your Sex Life.* New York: Simon and Schuster, 2015.

Neff, Kristen. *Self-Compassion: The Proven Power of Being Kind to Yourself.* New York: HarperCollins, 2011.

Neumann, Erich. *Depth Psychology and a New Ethic.* Boulder, CO: Shambhala, 1949.

Oliver, Mary. *House of Light: Poems by Mary Oliver.* Boston: Beacon Press, 2012.

O'Neill, Tom and Dan Piepenbring. *Chaos: Charles Manson, the CIA, and the Secret History of the Sixties.* New York: Little, Brown and Company, 2019.

Rees, Anuschka. *Beyond Beautiful: A Practical Guide to Being Happy, Confident, and You in a Looks-Obsessed World.* Berkeley, CA: Ten Speed Press, 2019.

Rinpoche, Sogyal. *The Tibetan Book of Living and Dying.* New York: HarperCollins, 1992.

Rumi. *The Essential Rumi: Translations by Coleman Barks.* New York: HarperOne, 2004.

Schucman, Helen. *A Course in Miracles.* New York: The Foundation for Inner Peace, 1976.

Silver, Tosha. *Outrageous Openness: Letting the Divine Take the Lead.* New York: Atria, 2014.

Taylor, Sonya Renee. *The Body is Not an Apology: The Power of Radical Self-Love.* Oakland, CA: Berrett-Koehler, 2018.

Thérèse, de Lisieux, Saint. *Story of a Soul: The Autobiography of Saint Thérèse of Lisieux.* Translated by John Clarke. Washington, DC: ICS Publications, 1976.

Teresa, Mother. *No Greater Love.* Novato, CA: New World Library, 1989.

Van Loon, Michelle. *Becoming Sage: Cultivating Meaning, Purpose, and Spirituality in Midlife.* Chicago: Moody Press, 2020: 165.

Walker, Matthew. *Why We Sleep: Unlocking the Power of Sleep and Dreams.* New York: Simon and Schuster, 2017.

Williamson, Marianne. *A Return to Love: Reflections on the Principles of A Course in Miracles.* New York: HarperPerennial, 1992.

Films

Heckerling, Amy, dir. *Clueless.* 1995; Paramount Pictures.

Kanisevska, Marek, dir. *Less Than Zero.* 20th Century Fox, 1987.

Smith, Chris, dir. *Fyre: The Greatest Party That Never Happened.* Netflix, 2019.

Tashlin, Frank, dir. *Will Success Spoil Rock Hunter?* 20th Century Fox, 1957.

Yates, David, dir. *Harry Potter and the Half-Blood Prince.* Warner Bros, 2009.